Return to Light
John of God Helps

Sam

Third Edition

Copyright SAM/Lightworker's Log

All rights reserved.

ISBN 978-1-939890-19-1

Brief quotations embodied in critical articles and reviews allowed. Include the book's title, author's name, and the Lightworker's Log website (LightworkersLog.com) as sources of further information. Contact the author via the above website to comment, for written permission regarding longer excerpts, or to otherwise use or reproduce this book.

Views expressed in this book are solely those of the author's perception at the time of writing. Channeled material flowed through the author in 2011 and 2012. The author of this book does not dispense medical advice or prescribe the use of any technique as a form of treatment for psychic, spiritual, physical, emotional, or medical problems without the advice of a physician. The intent of the author is only to share her experience and offer information of a general nature to help you in your quest for spiritual and emotional well-being. In the event you use any of the information in this book, the author, publisher, website host, and all parties associated with the book are not responsible for your actions.

Because of the dynamic nature of the Internet, Web addresses or links contained in this book may have changed since publication and may no longer be valid.

This book is dedicated to *All That Is*, the Divine Light within humanity. Divine Light shines brightly, ever glowing, for humanity to recognize and reap the benefits of Oneness.

Acknowledgements

Everyone noted within these pages helped me to recognize my true self, the Self of *All That Is*.

Reverend Steve Hooks and Reverend Ernie Chu made it possible to experience this journey filled with grace and ease. I would not hesitate to recommend them as companions for a trip to Casa de Dom Inacio (House of Saint Ignatius).

Boundless love and gratitude forever flows toward Medium Joao Teixeira de Faria, known as John of God, and our guide Vinicius Turki – Guide to Casa de Dom Inacio for helping me to verify that the time to let go of old energies is here.

Heartfelt appreciation goes to many named, and unnamed, companions met during the journey. You are a wonderful part of me and it was truly a joy to spend time with you basking in the energies of Oneness.

Contents

Introduction			ix
Chapter			
	1	*The Journey Begins*	1
	2	*Entering the Flow*	13
	3	*Continued Blessings*	33
	4	*Shades of Dilemma*	51
	5	*Off to Pirenopolis*	61
	6	*Surrender at Last*	71
	7	*Blessings Abound*	95
Epilogue			107
Perfecting the Lightbody			111
About the Author			117

Introduction

The Casa de Dom Inacio (Casa) draws people from all avenues of life. Many feel a variety of dis-ease and come as a last resort. Some may not believe in what many people refer to as God but have exhausted, or so they believe, all healing possibilities. People may visit after learning of healing miracles to experience healing, accompany others, or out of curiosity. And then there are those who come habitually to share their unique energy.

News of the Casa draws some individuals for unknown reasons while others may know they visit to boost their Light quotient. Yes, some of us believe we are returning to forms of Divine Light left behind eons ago, upon deciding to become humans with denser bodies. We now consciously take in Light to become more ethereal each day.

Most people truly believe world-renowned Brazilian healer and Medium, Joao Teixeira de Faria, known as John of God, heals various disorders known only to man. The truth is, through a variety of unseen entities, John of God helps people to be more in harmony with Higher Self. As a channel to higher realms, John of God helps souls calibrate and become more in harmony with the One of *All That Is*. For, in essence, we are parts of *All That Is* who have forgotten our true and Divine Nature to change all circumstances to our liking.

I booked this adventure sans research thinking it was merely a trip to Brazil with friends. And after booking the tour, and learning a bit about John of God, the thought of helping others spurred me on. And yet, this world, as many are beginning to know, is illusory in nature. It consists of vibrant consciousness that interacts with thoughts, deeds, and actions taken by many lost in the dream of separation.

My brain wants to sort everything out and write in the usual subsequent fashion. But another part of me often finds that words flow, quickly running from mind to hand, as an expression of *All That Is* directs. This type of writing is not new to me but today offers the first opportunity to channel a work somewhat not of this world.

This book contains current thoughts and channeled messages (from *Book of One :-) Volume 2*) in *italics*. Quote marks in *italics* signify channeled messages.

The Truth of *All That Is* rests safely within our heart's core and as the following message notes, we need only tap into this Source of Perfection to be free of disease.

*"In Truth, there is no separation of BEing but only the seamless Whole of Perfection. This Truth is becoming more evident as each day passes into nights of **All That Is**. Many dream of the realms beyond earth life and know there is something more. Many know, without a doubt, that this is the land of play, the place to experience, express, and expand while continuing to be a part of the Whole of **All That Is**.*

*"There is nothing outside of this whole. But the light of One continues to strive and keep all in the darkness of being alone in the experience. This is a necessary process for all to recognize their own true power, the power of **All That Is**, which lies inside of the keepers of One. The layers to humanities separation are cumbersome, and dispelling, for all who attempt to find the trueness of One. Let them fade into the darkness of nothing from whence they came. Focus on the Light of*

*Truth, the **All That Is**, which resides within each seemingly separate part of the Whole.*

*"This Light is everlasting and quells all thought of separation when in tune with **All That Is**. John of God helps those that wish to calibrate and harmonize consciously and those who wish healing on other levels. It is all the same. The calibration and harmonizations occurs regardless of the aspirants' readiness or ability to recognize it.*

*"All things in time, and all time in things of earth. For this truth, we leave the Whole of One to play in the darkness of a much smaller part of Self. This fact, as all others on earth, is an untruth known only to man. Earth beings are of a certain vibration that must calibrate and harmonize back to the Oneness of BEing. That Oneness of BEing is **All That Is**, a perfection of Wholeness and the only Truth that exists. Although we may ramble on, there is an essence we wish to convey.*

*"The Truth of **All That Is** lies within each figment of the Whole. That Truth is known, and revealed further, as the one of separation asks to receive it."*

Chapter One

The Journey Begins

"We must always have trustworthy and reliable men in positions of responsibility, but instead of looking to them for integrity, loyalty, and fidelity, we must look to the Spirit that animates them, and all men, to perform Its functions." Joel S. Goldsmith – Living The Infinite Way

My mind wanders aimlessly as the plane soars though blue skies on June 12, 2011. A window seat places me next to what some would call a mysterious stranger. She exudes an air of elegance and chats in Portuguese with the friendly, male, airline attendant as I put headphones on to hear the movie. The radio channel switches unexpectedly to Katy Perry's song "Firework." Daniel's essence fills the air as Katy sings.

"You just gotta ignite the Light and let it shine. Just own the night like the 4th of July."

How wonderful it feels to accept this blessing from the spirit of my last-born son! There's no doubt. I'm indeed in the right place at the appropriate time. Leaning forward, I poke Steve's shoulder to report the incident. He turns slowly, smiling to announce the correct channel.

The non-stop flight arrives in Brasília, Brazil after two meals and three movies. It's been an amazingly delightful flight, which seems shorter in duration than expected. Our small tour group disembarks before moving through customs. A relatively short line for foreigners delights because other lines are longer. Within minutes, a tall, dark, handsome guide directs us to a small motorcoach near curbside. Vinicius Turki – Guide to Casa de Dom Inacio – radiates a familiar wave of spiritual alignment, which I'm pleased to recognize.

In time for bed ninety minutes later, we turn onto a narrow, darkened street in Abadiania. This small town clearly "rolls up the sidewalks," much earlier than many others. The small, motorcoach stops in front of a darkened Pousada (hotel). A large, muscular man rises from his perch on a chair to open a white, iron gate leading to the small lobby.

Minutes later, discomfort overwhelms while standing in a smelly room. The current body that hosts this soul has never been to Brazil so there's no way to determine if my garden room is standard. Confusion abounds. Do I really want to stay in a room that reeks of limitation? It seems entirely unsuitable after spending more than fifty years to move out of squalor. This room is large, sparsely appointed, and smells strongly of bug spray. Two beds, a footstool, and an old, metal stand sit on the dirty floor.

The bathroom, thankfully, has a sink, shower, and regular toilet sitting on top of a block of concrete, like a throne. There are no shelves or cabinets, just a single hook by the door, towel holders, and a crude clothesline where most shower curtains sit. A single, thin bath towel looks hardly enough to dry one after bathing.

Although chilly air flows in through the bathroom window, I leave it open while taking a shower because the familiar, toxic smell of bug spray engulfs me. Water flows onto the toilet, and all over the floor, but it doesn't matter. It's all I can do to force myself to stay under a stream of cold water long enough to wash sweat from a day's travel. Will there ever be hot water?

The Journey Begins

There are no fans to clear the air so I'm grateful for another small, open window in the bedroom. Dust fills my nostrils upon leaning down to place moccasin slippers on the floor. The thought of unpacking leaves me cold. I place my small suitcase below a wooden rod, on a middle shelf. After hanging the next day's clothes on hangers, I zip up the larger suitcase before placing it on the top shelf.

Threadbare bedsheets look dirty so I lie on the top one. Familiar, jagged flashes of white light occasionally fill vision as I toss and turn upon the new, thin mattress. Warm, wooly socks keep feet toasty as the temperature drops below my usual comfort zone of 72-78 degrees. Working during hours of sleep, as a Lightworker, is now my usual practice. Generally when traveling on the first night, it's difficult to fall asleep.

Consciousness whisks me away to other lives where I transmute negative aspects of the little soul, much of the time. Sometimes I help people currently immersed in the dramas of this human life. And always, upon rising, during naps, and on the cusp of sleep, I consciously draw in the Light. Clearly, that routine will not work here where I must be awake and alert to suit the tour's itinerary. I decide to work the day shift while in Abadiania for it's customary to be in bed ten to fourteen hours a day.

Sleep comes many hours later, two hours before it's time to rise. Another opportunity to move out of my Light filled comfort zone of solitude, to practice the state of BEing with others, soon dawns. Voices fill the air as people wander into the open-air dining room three yards from my door. I rise upon hearing the familiar laugh of someone from our group at seven o'clock in the morning. It's five hours before my usual rising time. For the first time in many weeks, I have not taken the time to draw

Light into every tissue, cell, organ, and fluid of my physical body.

"Humanity must take on new forms to withstand the changes now occurring upon Mother Earth. The Lightbody is the only important body to concentrate upon as we morph DNA to align more closely with our original form. Lightworker's, wayshowers, and starseeds pave the way for humanity in this regard as they knowingly expand Light within physical frames.

"This morphing of physicality will take a bit of time for humanity but those already morphing knowingly will reach the point of expanded BEing sooner than the rest of humanity. Make no mistake; the morphing of DNA occurs regardless of the aspirant's ability to recognize changes.

"As humanity moves though this process to revert to original form, know that all is well. There has never been a separation, of any sort, in **All That Is**. As soul's you have taken on these false images and as souls you must revert to original, pure form, the perfect form of Light and Wholeness."

An air of adventure and excitement permeates the area as I wander out to the buffet line. Bowls of fresh, organic fruit (papaya, watermelon, pineapple, and banana) sit amid plates of white cheese and white bread. Another table holds a variety of cookies made with white flour, jars of healthy grains, and drinks. This is, I soon learn, the standard breakfast for our Pousada.

The area fills with people who came for a variety of reasons. Many know why they are here but a good portion wonder until they feel the energies of Oneness. Some people have an urgent request for healing while others express minor aliments. Individuals receive healing

The Journey Begins

Casa energies often without recognition of a change occurring. Those inextricably drawn to either participate in healing energies or move though them easily, to clear discarnate energies, are harder to identify.

Sharing meals, after living alone, is a pleasure. But I remain silent as each person shares his or her story. Everyone, it seems, is here to bask in the healing energies of the Casa, to heal dis-ease. Possessing little knowledge of the Casa or John of God, I came, or so I believe, to vacation in another country with friends. It's somewhat difficult to stay silent as those desperate for a miracle cure speak.

John of God allows numerous entities (healing spirits) to use his physical host and heal individuals through spiritual intervention. Since I consider my own physical host perfect, there is nothing to heal. Furthermore, if there were something to heal, I would not ask someone to heal me but use the Power within to co-create perfection, just as I have these past five years.

Doubts burst forth. Why am I here? It seems as if everyone is giving away their power as unlimited co-creators to seek healing from something outside of them. Having experienced multiple healings over the past several years, I'm not willing to surrender responsibility for myself. I know the Power of *All That Is* resides within ready to manifest conditions and experiences. Perhaps, I'm here to complement healing energies and help everyone recognize their true nature as unlimited co-creators. This seems reasonable.

"Now it's becoming more easier to meld with the powers that be. The richness you serve to enrich is ever fuller as the extent of your wholeness becomes well known to many more upon this planet. The Wholeness within you spreads out to all those surrounding in, above, through

the earth. Humanity's proxies live wholly and fully in the moment of Now. Their life, no longer a true measure of the human form now left behind, they go forth and spread the word of One to all who care to listen."

The Power of *All That Is* works though me to assure that numerous physical imperfections, treasures of ego, no longer motivate this physical host. Yes, it took nearly sixty years to learn that I AM the Creator of my own destiny. I AM the molder of thought, and body, and now choose Divine Perfection to motivate thoughts, words, and deeds. I AM entirely responsible for every facet of this life and despite physical appearances; there is nothing outside of me. The Divine Spark of *All That Is* resides within the core of my heart and I call it forth at will. It is a heady thought, which I often fail to share for numerous reasons.

All thoughts feed the Matrix in which we live. Affirmations, spoken clearly without naming a specific dis-ease, work best. It's always agreeable to note alignment with *All That Is*, perfection in all senses, and that is what I do now. I am not ready to surrender to any power recognized by many as outside of the little self. Recognition that this is yet another aspect of the greater part of my essence escapes me.

"The richness of **All That Is** awaits the pleasure of your company in what you refer to as 'Heaven.' This is not a physical place, per se, but a state of consciousness that all exist in now. You have only to change your current state of consciousness to dwell there in all aspects. Allowing yourself this pleasure is easy if you concentrate wholly on the One within each and every being.

"The times before humanity now appear as changing states of awareness, in which all will eventually *blossom forth, into knowing states of their own awareness as perfect, whole beings, capable of bearing the Light and making their own world. In these times of seeming uncertainty, you have many on the planet that wish to continue playing the game of separation, disillusionment, and woe. This game is reaching it's end very quickly as many learn there are many more games to play, new games in other realities of BEing. Old souls know the truth of this and are quickly moving in mass to play these new games. And yet, need I remind you, all is illusion.*

"*The state in which your True Self exists is one of unchanging Love, Light, and Truth. It is a place of caressing, eternally, all who dwell there, for it is the only place to dwell. All games played on other realms of existence, in other seeming times and spaces, are but shadows of wanting to be something of which no one being is.*

"*All exist in the knowing consciousness of One within* **All That Is***. To clarify, humanity is but a part of the One that exists in* **All That Is***, yet that One is but one figment of many, many entities making up the whole of* **All That Is***.*

"*We bid you good day knowing that the channel though which we speak is growing in greater consciousness here in this space and time.*"

This experience is my opportunity to hold more Light within a physical frame. The reservations fell easily into place after receiving Steve's email announcing the trip. Since I nurture new ways of living, it's not easy to make arrangements for a trip out of town. Timeworn energies are largely a thing of the past. Credit cards and checks are no longer a steady part of my world. I prefer to use cash when possible. Steve took care of all arrangements. The only thing I had to do was greet him, at the doorstep of my sanctuary, with bags packed for the trip to Miami International Airport.

As usual, after seeking advice from the Divine Spark within, I sensed my task was to join the group to "help" and "bump it up." Trips taken over the past few years offered various opportunities to help individuals through Divine Order and Divine Timing. There's no reason to believe I will not be of service during this grand adventure.

In the back of my mind, I think of an eye issue where sometimes there's difficulty seeing. A renowned eye specialist diagnosed floaters in January 2008 when I asked him to check for retinal tears. At that time, in addition to seeing flashes of light associated with spiritual awakening, floaters, within a mass of gray film, sometimes completely covered right eye vision. They still sporadically appear to block vision. The issue now seems worse than before. And at certain times, there's a long line of white light sporadically in my right eye. "Just being at the Casa," I think, "may help to manifest clear vision." I have no idea that light episodes such as this are normal for those holding more Divine Light.

One may see sporadic flashes of light, pinpoints of light, and lines of white light as the body increases its vibrational rate. After all, the human form is returning to the Light form left eons ago. But feel free to seek medical advice if this happens to you and you resonate with those energies.

A sense of community permeates the entire town making me feel comfortably welcome. As our group ventures out for a view of the Casa, I stop at the tiny, front desk. The manager agrees to send someone to clean the dirty floor in my room. Crisp air accompanies us as

The Journey Begins

we stroll down the narrow, concrete street, past tiny shops and Pousadas. Perfect weather is a welcome relief from the heat and humidity of South Florida. It's in the sixties and I'm wearing my sweater for the first time in ages.

Casa grounds are open to the public seven days a week. John of God greets masses of people Wednesday through Friday. Freshly painted, blue, iron gates stand wide open, less than a block from our Pousada, to welcome us on this beautiful Monday morning. Several painters slap blue and white paint on walls as Ernie and Steve explain. It is in preparation for the year's special event, a birthday party to celebrate Joao's birth.

Freshly painted Casa walls

After listening to explanations of how the Casa usually operates, I head to the bookstore to make crystal bed appointments. Crystals cleanse and help to balance our Chakra energies. Entities often 'prescribe' sessions for individuals seeking spiritual intervention. Luxuriating beneath an array of specially cut and lighted quartz crystals is my top priority for some unknown reason. Curiosity spurred me to list it as a 'must do' during my Casa visit. The small price of about $13 in American money makes sessions a bargain.

The Crystal Bed is a healing system using seven quartz crystals positioned over Chakra centers. Some individuals note inter-dimensional effects resulting in vibrational patterns that manifest higher levels of peace, awareness, and harmony. The vibration resonating from crystals affects the water in our bodies, positively affecting health. Of course, the more we think about something, the more firmly it manifests in our world.

A tourist caresses several small, wooden triangles as I pay for sessions. Days later, I'll learn that people use them to communicate with Casa entities.

Crystals outside the Casa bookstore

My first twenty-minute session in Room 7 refreshes hours later. Soothing music fills the room and a tingling sensation permeates my chakras. A familiar force field of energy surrounds me right before the room attendant opens the door. I look forward to tomorrow's session while purchasing bottles of blessed water and crystals from the bookstore.

No one has to convince me of the value assigned to blessed water for I know about the scientific studies of Japanese scientist, Masuro Emoto. Emoto showed, in graphic form, that words change the structure of water reorganizing it around minerals and the vibration of words and thoughts. Yes, the properties of water change with positive or negative intention. By ingesting blessed water, we offer the human body opportunities to mend and heal dis-ease. Water blessed with love and gratitude creates a perfect tool to help anyone raise his or her vibrational rate to heal dis-ease.

New energies abound but I have difficulty staying in tune with them. I so want to stay in the habit of reporting events as they happen and yet, these energies prompt me to change my ways, to work with new energies I have yet to master.

The portable CD player sticks on a song as I begin to fix dinner. It's a sign that a message is forthcoming...

The message is for the masses, which I often think are outside, but are really within the ego of the lower self. I write for myself and no one else for I am truly alone in this world of luxury. There is no time to speak of, no tasks to complete, as long as I stay fixed within my own domain, away from the common pleasures of physicality.

These pleasures no longer interest me unless, of course, I am traveling to distant places, experiencing new things with people of like-mind. The patterns of yesterday have faded but new patterns appear to take their place. I often wonder when, or if, these new patterns will fly in the world as those of yesteryear.

"Enough already," I hear from the voice within.

"You must concentrate on getting the message out even if you think that message is solely for you. There is only One in which you live, and move, and have all BEing and it is truly time to gather in the fold. This is a momentous time for all humanity, as earth changes make many consider other possibilities, while removing comfort zones of past lives. This is indeed a great time of change and all must master the newness of energies as yet unrecognized by the masses. All will hearken to these promptings very soon as the summer months wear away old energies and thoughts of old.

"There is a New Order in town and that New Order is not the world order some believe will rule. This New Order is one of Love and Light, of Truth and Security for all, of Abundance and Joy for all living on earth. It is not exclusive and includes all who walk upon the earth. This is the time of mass uprisings in the masses of unawakened beings of Light, who soon, through their own efforts, will recognize the Truth of Oneness. I leave you with this thought.

"What will you do when the world changes beyond your own recognition?"

Chapter Two

Entering the Flow

The mental atmosphere that surrounds us is impressed not only with the thoughts and feelings we create, but the thoughts and feelings of those around us. James Van Praagh – Reaching to Heaven

Vivid dreams, lately the rule rather than the exception, take me far away while napping in my bleach-permeated room. Sensing spirits upon waking ninety minutes later, I know the current session of transmuting negative energy, from past lives, is now complete.

Clear, blue skies bless this beautiful day when group members pile into a taxi in the late afternoon. The ordinary looking, small car, without meter or commercial signs, is much different from those in the U.S. Nearly a mile later, our driver maneuvers through a large group of hiking tourists, a city block from the local healing waterfall. Appealing temperatures add to immense gratitude as we move ahead of the crowd.

Several people stand in line before us. Steve explains the protocol as the taxi driver pulls away. There are two entries to pass through. We should wait at the first until a few people move out after having their experience. The large group of tourists round the bend as Steve continues to talk.

This is a sacred place requiring silence once we pass through the first entry. Men and women are to enter the second area separately. We should join with others to enhance our own experience and shorten the line for those still waiting. Couples are the exception. When we reach the gate, we are to wait until those before us pass back through, after experiencing the waterfall's healing effects.

The noisy, large, tourist group moves quickly ahead, talking in a language I don't understand, as we look on, astonished at their lack of protocol. It now takes much longer to accomplish our mission.

A vivacious, American woman pushes her way through the line to reach us twenty minutes later. She asks to join our group of three women and immediately begins a long conversation about area hotels. Maria and this woman engage in several minutes of excited conversation as she recounts her journey after staying longer than expected. There's no doubt, in my mind, that unseen forces paved the way for her to speak with us. I sit or stand quietly as she answers Maria's questions.

We move through the gate in silence when it's finally our turn to relish in healing waters. The water is icy cold. "Perhaps," I think, "it's even colder than frigid waters of the Gallatin River in Yellowstone." Although I do not wish to prolong time here, intuition guides to dunk my head under the icy cold stream, three times. I do so with a yelp before returning to companions to don my cover up.

It's now time to bestow a blessing upon the American stranger. This is my job for today. My arms reach out after she pulls her clothes on over a colorful, two-piece swimsuit. I hug her warmly, pushing out Love and Light from within, as she returns the hug. A quick message flows out of my mouth but I forget it immediately. The hug is much longer than expected and she is clearly appreciative when we stop to thank one another. Maria and Cathy are now hugging as well.

Entering the Flow

One squiggly, double-line of spirit energy graces a photo of statues sitting two yards from my Pousada door hours later. Several familiar looking orbs of spirit energy appear in the empty field across from the Casa after dinner. The nearly full moon offers more opportunities to capture spirit energy as we walk towards Café Central.

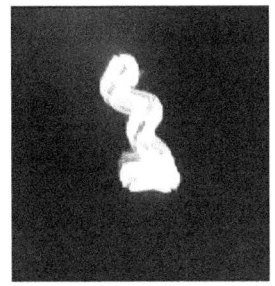

Grainne greets us warmly, happy to see Steve and Ernie again. Her husband Joao takes our orders for Acai Pudding (a fruit delight in much demand for its healing properties), dandelion coffee, chocolate chip cookies, milkshakes, and chocolate cake. The atmosphere is alive with excitement and new beginnings as everyone shares their day.

A cold shower again chills me before bedtime. Even though the showerhead is set on hot water, none comes out of the stream. Warm pajamas prompt immense gratitude before crawling onto the full-size bed.

Hours of restless sleep follow. A message breaks through the veil between three and four o'clock in the morning. I rise to capture several pictures but fail to document the message, which is highly unusual for me. My small tape recorder remains packed away so the message is soon forgotten. Digital pictures show the faint colors of a rainbow in my room!

Dawn breaks on the horizon. Although sleep deficient, based on usual habits, it's easier to rise today. We are free to enjoy our own adventures until the evening. I pull on sneakers to walk after breakfast. The cheerful front desk clerk listens politely as I ask for clean sheets before heading toward the Casa. He nods and says there is a new housekeeper to meet all needs.

Sun sits, amid solid blue skies, inviting me to take a picture. A series of unfamiliar orbs appears on the camera's display as I gaze in awe. Something that reminds me of the blessed Mother Mary floats among alternating, white, pale blue, and magenta colored orbs. It's the first time I capture such an anomaly.

Workers continue to paint various areas of the Casa as I skirt around roped off sections amid few tourists. Statues present another photo opportunity but I'm disappointed when nothing out of the ordinary appears. I leave Casa grounds to head further down the road, away from town.

Concrete ends abruptly at the Casa property line. Now the crunch of dirt fills the air as sneakers squash bits and pieces of red earth, rocks, and road debris. Within minutes, the muscles in my legs ache. My breathing becomes labored. I have not walked for weeks and the combination of a higher altitude, mixed with moving up small hills, wears me out.

Entering the Flow

A branch of three paths lies ahead. Fireworks fill the air; at least I hope it's the noise that surrounds me. I continue forward for the other two paths lead a long, way, downhill. It's inconceivable to expend the energy required to climb back up them to return. The narrow, dirt road ends at the top of the second, small hill. It's merely a few blocks from the Pousada. I stand to take in the glory of Nature breathing in cooler air. A contrast of dry earth and weeds, coupled with rolling green fields below, offers another perfect photo opportunity before heading back to my room for a nap.

Lunch consists of colorful, fresh, organic vegetables, fruit, white bread, rice, chicken, stewed vegetables, and beef. All the fresh vegetables are finely sliced, diced, grated, or chopped. I try a bit of each. It's the first time I eat fresh beets, instead of drinking them as part of a health food drink.

*"Bodies continue to morph to become more in tune with **All That Is**. Let this not dissuade you from knowing that all is in Divine Order as the body morphs more each day. Continuing to follow a regimen of live, organic foods, slight exercise, and meditation, filled with gratitude, helps to capture the essence within, as all continue on this journey back to Oneness in all aspects.*

*"Each personality bears it's own symptoms of the change. But be aware that all body systems are affected by the increasing energies that assault your earth. Mother Gaia continues to purge all that is not in tune with the wonder of **All That Is**. This becomes increasingly apparent to those living in the west and mid-section of your world.*

"Bearing the Light of Oneness, during all events, helps to merge with the Truth of BEing in all aspects. Fear not as these changes become more apparent and

*undeniable to many in your world. Those safe in the arms of **All That Is** shall continue to lead the way though the darkness of this illusory period of time."*

    Maria and I walk back to the Casa after lunch for Crystal Bed sessions. This second session is much more amazing than the first. A cool mist seems to cover my body as soothing music fills the air. It's at the point when the music takes one on a trip to a tropical rain forest where light rain begins to fall. The busy attendant politely smiles when I thank her in Portuguese before leaving to book another session for tomorrow.

    A friendly American woman stops to chat as I sit in the open-air dining room transferring photos from a Smart Card to my new, tiny, travel laptop. She seems very in tune with Casa energies and reports that her stay ended up longer than expected. "Am I meant to stay longer than expected too?" I ponder, recalling that this is the second person in two days to note such an occurrence. We immediately strike up a conversation about spirit energy as I show her various orb pictures. Before Faye moves on, she reminds me my soul has brought me here for a reason. Regardless of what I believe, it would be best to surrender to Casa energies.

    Vinicius meets our tour group in the lobby for the next adventure, a trip to dinner at an all you can eat Brazilian meat restaurant. It's a short but pleasant drive to an area much more commercialized than Abadiania. Promises of Buffalo steak fill my head when we enter the nearly empty, elegant restaurant less than an hour later. Surrounding energies are much different here. Obviously, customs are different too as owners use quality napkins for show rather than a customer's use. Waiters replace lovely, colorful, cloth napkins with plain white paper ones as soon as we take our seats.

Entering the Flow

Children play in an adjoining room, amid various games and playhouses, while waiters offer endless cuts of meat. It all seems highly spiced and hard to chew. The meat, in my estimation, is substandard, for now I only eat filet mignon or ground Buffalo, grass-fed, free of hormones or other additives now commonly given to animals in the U.S. There's no Buffalo but I do enjoy the array of cheeses and other condiments.

Vinicius speaks to us separately after dinner to discuss plans for the following day, our first day at the Casa with John of God. Most people ask for something to heal when they go though the line. Some people purchase and take herbs prescribed by entities working though John of God before coming here. Our wise guide seems to understand when I say there's nothing to heal. He nods as I announce my goal of returning to the Lightbody.

"Yes," Vinicius agrees solemnly, while writing on a small sheet of white paper. "This world is illusion and it is as you believe."

"All things subsist within the time and space of your world. Know that thought is the basis of your reality and fill your mind with those thoughts that you wish to keep. To mold a better life for others, and yourself, you must concentrate on life-affirming thoughts that allow you to claim the power you relinquished eons ago.

"As the time and space within your world changes we offer words of wisdom for your consideration. Speaking within the ethers of your time and space becomes easier as gross changes take place upon your earth. These changes make it easier for us, from the immaterial world, to focus more closely on your reality. All thought is manifested on some level of space and time. And yet, there are no thoughts beyond the ethers of your

world, for your world is the only world within the reality of time and space.

"Make your world with your thoughts of wholeness and peace (such as):

"I am my I AM Presence, perfect, whole and free, always having the best possible experience."

Vinicius offers me a blue, plastic covered 'ticket' with the slip of paper. Tomorrow, he explains, I will hand the blue 'ticket' to the monitor while moving through the First Time Line. Vinicius will soon accept the slip of paper to remind him of my request when I stand before John of God.

Wednesday morning brings unexpected joint aches and pains, a reminder of incurable osteoarthritis requiring loads of medications up until some time in 2006. My intestines hurt as well. I rise early to join those who talk excitedly of today's adventure. Some will move through the Second Time Line because they took prescribed, Casa herbs (passion flower permeated with the energies of each request) before their arrival.

Ernie and Steve are the only ones in our group who are not here for the first time. We walk together down the concrete road among lots of people, of various ages, shortly before eight o'clock in the morning. Everyone wears white clothing. Some say the entities request it because it's easier for them to work on people. I'm beginning to understand that it's a great equalizer for no one stands out in the crowd, except for those in wheelchairs.

Steve leads us in through the rarely used entrance on the side of the building. The large, open-air, waiting room already holds many people. There are no seats near us or at the front of the room. The crowd parts as we

Entering the Flow

make our way worming around wheelchairs. People stand or sit outside filling the area nearby. We move to the back wall, near the main entrance, where a few of us eventually find seats on a concrete bench. It's impossible to see the stage for a solid line of people stand in the small space between the last wooden bench and us.

A speaker comes onto the stage shortly after 8:00 AM. For the next few minutes, he explains Casa rules in Portuguese, English, and other languages. People approach the stage to place slips of paper within the large wooden triangle on the wall behind him. Some linger as they raise their arms to grip the wall while their forehead rests within the center. Despite what I see as a disruption, the tall, thin man does a good job of continuing his task, unmoved by the steady stream behind him.

My hand rises when he asks who is here for the First Time Line. Several workers roam the area taking count of people there with hand counters. Clearly adept at their task, they move quickly through the room while scanning for raised hands. There are fewer people to move through the Second Time Line.

Someone interrupts the speaker after several minutes. He soon announces that those who have come for "operation" may now form a line near the entrance. Another speaker takes the stage. She speaks in a language I don't understand. We know she calls for the First Time Line when Steve nods for us to rise and join the procession. Minutes later, the line stops flowing. Vinicius appears suddenly to motion us forward.

It all seems very surreal with hordes of people seeking a miracle of healing. The speaker continues to lead the crowd through a series of prayers. Each prayer changes the energy within the room, making it more positive and conductive to healing.

Prayers in foreign languages fill me with ease and grace because I don't understand the words. But those spoken in American no longer resonate with my soul. Structured religion has a way of keeping the masses set on looking outside themselves for someone else to take responsibility. Years of experiences, with unseen forces of Light, served to enlighten me to the truth that humanity is, and always has been, powerful enough to right all perceived "wrongs." We are much more powerful than we can ever know while in human form. Of this, I am certain.

"As higher vibrational energies continue to pummel the planet on which you live it is now vital to assimilate them with ease and grace. Those not accustomed to caring for their human host will experience various degrees of dis-ease unless they change their habits. The world now changes at a steady pace paving the way for progression of Soul. Everyone on earth is involved in this new game whether they know it or not.

"These days of increased consciousness continue to bring greater and greater possibilities for humankind to morph into a new sovereign being. There are some who do not wish this to happen for their game is an old one of manipulation and control. Be aware that as things increasingly become lighter, as energies continually change on your earth, these older, denser energies may appear to become even denser. But you must continue to be aware that this too is illusion, for those wanting to continue the old ways of yore know those ways are already vastly outdated.

"Your earth will experience many changes in the days ahead. Many of these changes will be products of the old crew's manipulation. But have faith for their manipulating ways will soon be known to all and stopped by mass consciousness. However, many souls agreed to be included in the aftereffects of these unwholesome

*changes. Know that all is going according to the Divine Plan of One as we move closer in Truth and BEing to **All That Is**."*

There is no savior in Heaven to heal me of my disease. I must take responsibility and hold the faith to do it myself. New prayers flow into my brain when speakers sprout familiar prayers. Walter Starke's revised Lord's Prayer from *It's All God*, adapted for my last book, springs forth to flow quickly through my brain.

My Inner Self, which art Heaven consciousness, wholly be thy recognition.

The kingdom of my Inner Self come, <u>Its</u> guidance be done at the outer material level as well as at the inner spiritual level.

My Inner Self, fulfill for me all my daily needs, body, mind, and Spirit.

Release me when I have not listened to my Inner Self as I release others who are not listening to theirs.

Lead me not into the temptation of believing my lower self is all; deliver me from the evil of believing I AM not already One.

For this realization of my Inner Self is Heaven, the only power, and the glory of all being.

And So It Is!

Repeated prayers noting the propensity to give ones power away begin to irritate me. Upon forgetting words to the revised Lord's Prayer, I switch to a version of *Amazing Grace* channeled months ago. A calm knowing of the Kingdom within overwhelms while singing the words in my head.

"*Amazing Grace, how sweet the sound, inside of everyone.*

"*Amazing Grace, how good to know, that there is only One.*

"*No one is lost. No one is found. No one can be apart.*

"*For every soul resides inside the place creation starts.*"

We soon gratefully leave, near the back of the long line, to wait near Vinicius at the entrance. He tells the monitor to allow us passage when the line begins again. Minutes later, we glide briskly through the first Current Room. Energies within this room are intense. It holds many people, sitting packed together on wooden benches with thin, blue padding. Their eyes are closed and they appear to be meditating. A middle-aged woman stands at the head of the room speaking softly.

"Keep your eyes closed." She tells them softly.

Those of us in line are to keep eyes open while staring straight ahead.

The next room is longer and we enter it from the middle. People meditating, while perched upon wooden benches, fill it too. Several people sit at the end of aisles in wheelchairs, also with eyes closed. John of God sits at the far end, beyond rows of what appear to be cushioned wooden chairs, on either side of the room. Each chair holds someone meditating with eyes closed. They, as others, add energy to that of Casa entities, to protect John of God from harm, and to complement healing energies flowing throughout Casa rooms.

The line moves very quickly. Movement through the building takes merely several minutes. Vinicius soon

Entering the Flow

steps back, from his spot near John of God, to take the white slip of paper from my hand. John of God, clearly "out to lunch," stares blankly as Vinicius explains my request. Vinicius hands me back the slip of paper and notes I am to receive a blessing. I am dazed, as if in a dream. A young woman quickly whisks me forward through another room filled with people meditating.

Another middle-aged woman motions me forward to sit among people in the last room, which I later learn is the Blessing Room. Several sit silently. Others cough, sneeze, or cry while the woman speaks in a foreign language. I follow the motions of those around me, close my eyes, and rise to leave when they do. Still trying to convince myself to surrender to Casa entities, I return to my room. This town, and everything in it, seems filled with controlling masculine energies. But perhaps, it's just my misperception.

"That of which you seek is already found, within you, within the heart's core sits all you need. Now is the time to focus on that wondrous BEing within. Let go of the world as your eyes envision it and take on the attributes of Oneness, pure, steady, and true.

"There is much to be said for waiting in silence for things to come to you. Know that this is not the time to be searching for answers to mundane questions of life for within you lay the answers to all you need know, now or ever."

Minutes later, upon remembering it's time for Blessed Soup, I head back to the Casa. Several members of my tour group welcome me into the quickly moving line. Vinicius pops out of the Casa to see if we have any questions. This afternoon, he tells me, I can sit in the Current Room or go in the Second Time Line. I opt for the Current Room. There's no desire to give my power away by asking for something from another. I'd much rather add Light-filled energies to the Casa flow.

We sit enjoying homemade soup while sharing experiences. The soup is absolutely delicious! It holds a variety of organic vegetables, noodles, and a few potatoes. Fresh cilantro reminds me of plants on the back porch in South Florida.

Many people fill the area. Some remain sitting in the main room, while others stroll around lush Casa grounds, meditating on wooden benches, or sharing experiences. This is clearly a nurturing atmosphere of physicality peppered with a community of like minds. Maria and I stop at the bookstore to purchase liters of mineral water blessed by the entities. After taking a few pictures of Casa statues, I head back to the Pousada for a hearty lunch.

Upon returning for my third Crystal Bed session, I envision an extra five minutes under the energies. The force field around my body comes sooner than previous days. Perhaps, my awareness of energy enhances the experience. Nevertheless, I enjoy the feeling until the attendant begins to open doors. She opens the door to my room just when I wonder if she's forgotten about me. It's exactly twenty-five minutes after the session began and I'm delighted to get my wish.

Entering the Flow

Fewer people fill the Casa waiting room during the afternoon session. A young Brazilian woman nods her head as I move quickly through the small doorway to sit in the first Current Room. As expected, an aisle seat, on a bench in the back, is empty. I sit down and close my eyes like everyone else.

The bench is very hard and soon my butt is uncomfortable. A young woman speaks softly as I try to concentrate on words instead of discomfort. We are clearly "on the same page" for her monologue resonates strongly. She talks of our true form, as Light, while reminding us to keep eyes closed. The lines begin. She thanks us for helping our brothers and sisters as they move though the line.

"The time is here for all to know the unity within. Focus on your own Self of One as each purges lower aspects. The time has come for all to know the glory of their True Self. This Self resides in each unique figment of humanity but needs to be brought forth at this crucial time for evolution.

"Knowing this Divine part of ones self helps to motor through upcoming changes, which shall affect all upon Mother Earth."

There's no mistaking surrounding positive, loving energies. These energies are the strongest I have ever felt, carrying me to a higher state of consciousness. Yet, my butt continues to ache. Sometimes I have difficultly concentrating on staying in the flow. Powerful and waning energies remind me of a roller coaster ride. Sometimes the energies are so intense that I cannot move an inch. Periodically, they vary, allowing me to change position.

Tuning out the few people crying softly soon becomes harder to do. Many people believe that as the line moves though the room any discarnate energy they may be holding could "attach" to those sitting in the room. That's one of the reasons why we are instructed to keep our eyes closed. I suspect closing the eyes also helps greatly to succumb to Casa energies, and move with positive flow, while adding to it.

Intuition tells me there's enough positive energy within my form to withstand any onslaught of discarnate energies. Against rules, I peek though silted eyes to sip water and follow the direction in my brain. Amid the periodic ebb and flow of intense energies, I shake my head and shoulders without a thought of what it may look like to those in the line. I try to wait until a break in the line to do so.

The session lasts for what seems like an eternity. In this reality, it's a bit more than two hours long. It pleases me beyond measure to feel I have made a difference in the energies, supporting those that came though the line. I soon hear that when we sit in 'Current' we are helping to heal the discarnate energy within our own soul as well.

"Those in lower levels of existence now break forth to live in greater states of awareness on this day. Earth's ethers thin allowing all who wish to do so, speak with their True Self (Higher Self). The Higher Self now leads all who wish to move forward into greater states of loving awareness. Letting go of the past as these energies surround earth serves one best. When you move forward, all are aboard to ride the train to freedom. Holding nothing back, all awaken as One, a Supreme Being of Love and Light.

Entering the Flow

"It's in the moment of not knowing that all things exist. The movement of Spirit is everywhere. You have only to tap into the Source. **All That Is** *reflects itself through everything you see, everything you do, and everything accomplished. There is no end to the aspects of* **All That Is** *as It marks the beginning of a new era, the era of Oneness for all humanity.*

"Take stock in the days ahead as we move forward toward the lightness of BEing. Many will not be able to withstand the pressures of this movement toward Wholeness. But make no mistake, the Truth of **All That Is** *lies within all living things. The works of One are within you. It is time to bring them out."*

After the beautiful monitor thanks us for our dedication, I stumble out of the Casa in a stupor. For the first time, I notice a convenience store near the exit. Intuition guides me to order a cup of orange juice from a young, Brazilian girl behind the counter. It takes several minutes to get because she squeezes the juice only upon an order. I watch amazed as the pretty girl cuts at least ten oranges to feed into a juicer. "This," I think drinking while regaining my composure upon a plastic, white chair, "is the best juice I've ever tasted."

Minutes later, I book another session on the Crystal Bed for tomorrow. The Casa experience is a venture I want to financially support and, for now, I can think of no better way than to buy more crystals for family members. Knowing some may not appreciate clear, exquisite, heart or peg-shaped stones, I purchase bracelets and triangle necklaces as well.

Our group is smaller for dinner this evening. Two members had psychic surgery so they must remain in their rooms for twenty-four hours. Someone Ernie met on a previous trip joins us. He soon announces that we must surrender to Casa entities when here. A mysterious rash covers his right leg.

"Have you ever seen such a thing?" He asks.

Dealing with increased energies now brings almost insatiable thirst, an inability to sleep, waking frequently after I finally do, and rising for the day with transmutation rashes upon my right cheek. Rashes on the lower legs are now a thing of the distant past.

Streets are dark and nearly empty as I stroll along the road with friends to Café Central later in the evening. Many people remain sequestered after surgery. As usual, our hosts are pleased to serve with smiles and jokes that make us roar with laughter.

The essence of Grainne at Café Central

After indulging in dandelion coffee, I return to sleep in my freshly made bed. The strange room hosts a wide crack under the door that allows easy entry for small creatures. Energies are rampant as I toss and turn. My travel candle goes out twice so I turn on a battery operated smiley face light. It makes me feel more comfortable to see the yellow smile. Something wakes me after three o'clock in the morning. Again, I sense Casa entities doing their thing as the smiley face light blinks.

"The times upon you now may seem awkward to many beginning to sense the constant onslaught of energies pummeling earth at this time. But be ye not afraid of the powers that fill humanity with readiness to receive what is yet to come, a much heftier onslaught of energies lies just beyond the horizon of today, your 12/11/12.

"This time will cease all operations wishing to coalesce into mass consciousness the fear of change. Change upon your earth will indeed occur but not as your mass media foretells. All will be in readiness to receive the tasks of Oneness as these energies come into your fields of Light.

"Letting nothing dissuade you from following the Truth of Oneness continues to be the best course to take to avoid humanity's woes of limitation and grief. Remember, there is nothing to stop you from achieving the greatest of your dreams but your own small self."

Chapter Three

Continued Blessings

There are no mistakes, no coincidences, all events are blessings given to us to learn from. Elizabeth Kubler-Ross

Severe, right hip pain accompanies mild joint discomfort, throughout my body, upon rising to greet Thursday morning. After a slow walk to Casa grounds, I take a seat in the Current Room. A heart crystal and triangle necklace graces my neck as I sit upon a sweater hoping to make today's session more comfortable.

Energies feel somewhat erratic but it's not quite the roller coaster ride of yesterday. Grainne reminds us periodically to keep eyes closed as she speaks of returning to Light. Casa energies quickly immerse as we blend gifts to form a healing, loving environment for brothers and sisters to relish in as they move through the room.

Grainne is very good about letting us know when there's a break in the line. I take advantage of those times to change position and sip from the blessed water near my side. The sweater doesn't seem to help but Casa energies lift me beyond this world's limitations, while giving in to go with the flow.

Today, there's less crying, coughing, and sneezing but somewhere, in the back of the room, a baby occasionally makes itself known. My head seems to spin occasionally, in a clock-wise motion, very quickly. The necklace sits in my sports bra less than three hours later. I have no idea how the double-knot untied itself! Are Casa energies telling me not to wear it during sessions of duty in the Current Room?

A strong sense of community envelops the line as those of us in service wait for Blessed Soup. People roam nearby sipping coconut water, from coconuts with straws, or enjoying ice cream bars from the convenience store. I feel privileged to sit among this community of love, taking more time to enjoy the soup before heading to the bookstore for more blessed water. An awesome reminder of Mother Mary again appears as I photograph the sun.

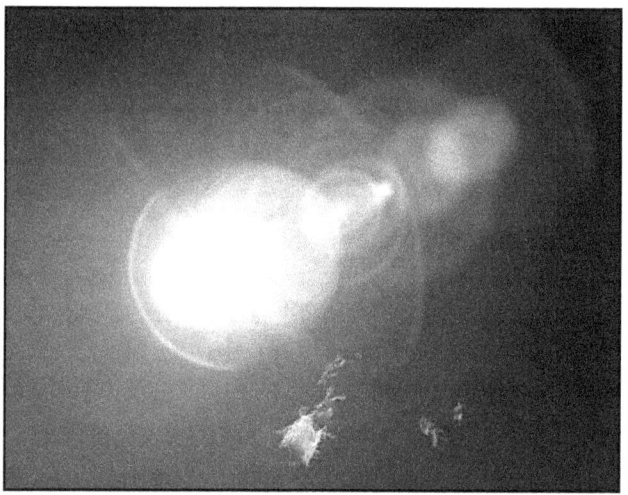

Gratitude abounds again at the pizza place when someone hands over laundry for cleaning later in the day. There's no need to wait four days to get clean underwear because I packed more than enough clothing for the two-week stay. My new friend and I find it odd that no one seems to know who does the laundry. Friendly, counter personnel take it for someone else to wash without knowing who completes the task.

Small pleasures fill me with immense joy for someone tells me to ask for "jello" when paying for a can of Diet Coke with B-complex vitamins. Finally, there's ice in my soda! Drinking Diet Coke is the only daily habit that remains from years of smoking, eating, and drinking unhealthy substances.

Back in my room for a nap after lunch, I consider moving through the line upon waking. Vision in my right eye seems cloudy. Could it be more than floaters diagnosed in 2008? Someone discussed eye disorders (cataracts) last night at dinner and now I take that spontaneous conversation as a sign. Both Dad and a sister had physical operations for cataracts. Momma, who transitioned weeks before I left for Brazil, experienced macular degeneration, which left her legally blind. I refuse to succumb to genetic dis-ease and remain steadfast against asking someone to heal me. Surely, this oddity will positively change, as other conditions, without asking for outside assistance.

Although I've successfully ignored what I refer to as America's "sick-care system" for four years, the thought of requiring eye surgery begins to surface. Paying ten-thousand dollars a year for health insurance to feed that system is no longer on my agenda. Returning to the system of old, unhealthy, controlling, and greedy energies is unthinkable. Yet, some people note it's unavoidable. Surgery is not a welcome thought so I push it out of my mind to proclaim body perfection, despite physical appearances.

*"All seek the richness of BEing very soon but few will hearken to the path's ways of depending only on what's held inside. Make no mistake as you go about your day. The Truth, the key to Life, dwells inside each living thing. There is nothing outside the spark of **All That Is**, which humanity holds inside each form.*

"Hearing only Truth serves humanity as this great leap of faith progresses. Keep nothing hidden as old systems, old ways of living, fall away. All shall know the

*glory and wonder of manifesting their heart's desire in coming years. But for now, most of humanity continues to sleep within the dream of dreams, as yet, unwilling to awaken. All shall continue to change more in tune with the One of **All That Is** as old systems fall away.*

*"The New Earth is already under your feet as these systems move away faster than imagined. Let nothing dissuade you from your Truth. For it is the very Truth of **All That Is**. You hold within your small Self of One the key to progressing."*

A choice to remain in the Heaven created with new energies in 2008 remains. Fear will not guide actions again. Guidance from Higher Self continues to come as needed. Of this, I am certain, and very grateful to avoid the "sick-care system." Although needed to help some return to wholeness, the old system energies mainly keep people in a body of ever-increasing dis-ease. I choose to return to Light and know the current aches and pains are in reality a sign of just that. I am taking in more, and more Light, as I transmute old energies from eons of soul disharmony!

Grainne guides us again during the afternoon session. This time I sit upon a pillow from the single bed in my room. Casa energies are totally different now. They are much more intense and rarely wane. My head spins like a top for most of the session and halfway through I wonder if anyone can detect the spin. So many extraordinary experiences happen to me, many of which I document in books, but this, this is something exquisitely new. For the first time in my life, I am having a delicious Merkaba experience. The forces are so strong that I think I may just float away. My neck aches when the session ends three and a half hours later.

Continued Blessings

There's no doubt. I could live in this community, relishing in Casa energies by day, sharing with like-minds, and moving to a higher state of BEing again at night. What a relief to know this! But my task in America is not complete. I am much more inclined to contribute in another unique way rather than support others in their unique efforts.

A short nap serves to refresh and brings another message. I am to go through the line tomorrow and relinquish the pictures in my wallet. All family photo albums remained with my ex-husband, three years ago, upon leaving the past behind to delve more deeply into the present moment. Two wallet photos of grandchildren remain because people thought it strange that I had no family pictures when everyone else was displaying theirs.

My companions and I discuss the decision at dinner.

*"The One of **All That Is** awaits your decision to grow in Truth, in Light, in the Love that you are. This requires stretching toward the unknown once again. The issues before humanity now strive to keep all locked into the game of separation. Buy not into that game but choose to play a game of your own.*

*"Strive toward feeling the Oneness of all things in all that you do. Take nothing for granted but the love of I AM for it is part of **All That Is**, which strives for recognition in this world.*

"Seek nothing outside the Oneness of your Self. Know that all things change quickly upon your earth to match the awareness of mass consciousness. Strive toward leaning that consciousness more into the Light of I AM. For that is the Truth of your BEing. The Light of I AM is ever ready to shine its brightness unto your world in new ways never seen nor experienced before."

"Perhaps it's a ploy," I announce, turning my head to address everyone, "to get me through the line again. I so prefer to stay in the Current Room, adding to and sharing the massive energy flow!"

More orb pictures of the Casa grace my cheap digital camera after dinner. Photos of an Italian invocation and statue of Our Lady of Montenero reveal the glory of spirit energies. A golden halo of light appears above the statues head. Blue mist flows below it within golden waves of energy. I return to the Pousada eager to show pictures to the others before dinner.

Vinicius takes us aside individually after dinner to discuss our experience. He reminds me that my soul led

Continued Blessings

me here for a reason when I tell him about my grandchildren's pictures. I agree to go through the Second Time Line with the photos in the morning. It's time to immerse myself more fully in the Casa experience.

Friday dawns as another beautiful day, with clear, blue skies and much cooler weather than South Florida currently enjoys. It's winter here in Brazil. Filled with a strong sense of gratitude, I rise to greet new friends and display photos at breakfast. My two grandchildren are wise beyond their years, in areas unknown to most humans. It shows clearly in the photo of Abigail at four years of age. No one correctly guesses her age. They all think she's eight-years-old.

Joint pain again accompanies me on my way to the Casa. (This is a normal occurrence during times of transmutation as we rid physicality of denser energies.) Seats in the waiting room fill with people from all walks of life. After making my way past the maze of wheelchairs and baby strollers, I spot the empty concrete space behind blue seats on the side of the room. Worming my way through the crowd seems easy.

After reaching the desired spot, I smile and motion to a woman sitting on concrete at the end of the row. Her knees are in the aisle because she cannot fit them in the tiny space in front of her. She looks at me with amused curiosity, for the row of seats in front of concrete spaces makes it impossible to pass easily behind them. A small Brazilian woman, who sits in front of her, smiles when I motion for her to lean forward. The space behind her opens just enough for me to squeeze through.

Seconds later, open palms sit on my thighs. Knees press into the tight space between two seats in front of me. Eyes close while sitting erectly to spread Light into the area as the speaker on stage begins to pray. He speaks in a foreign language making prayers sound soothing and exotic.

It seems like eternity before a speaker calls forth the second line. The woman is no longer beside me as I rise easily upon seeing people with tickets similar to mine. "If there is truly something seriously wrong with my eyes," I think while worming through the mass, "the entities will know when I present these pictures."

The first Current Room pulsates with erratic energy as the line moves quickly forward. Vinicius soon takes the pictures from my hand to present to John of God, who is again "out to lunch." His eyes are blank as he scribbles on two sheets of white paper. Vinicius takes the paper and hands it to me along with the pictures.

"Receive a blessing and return at 2:00 PM," he announces before a woman motions me away.

Intense emotion spurts forth to immediately overwhelm me.

"Why don't people recognize their true nature?" I lament, moving toward the Blessing Room.

Tears begin to rise. They spill out onto cheeks as I sit listening to the soft voice of a French Canadian woman speaking English. Truly, I do not understand, but must accept that my soul knows best.

"The times they are a' changing for the better or the worse depending upon what reality you focus on. Keep your thoughts on the 5-D reality of experience. Focus your thoughts on the Love and Light of the 5-D reality to experience the better.

"That of which I AM is steadfast Truth waiting to break through the ethers of the ethereal realm into this physical world. That of which I AM is ready to do so for *the Truth shines brightly for those within the Light of One.*

*"Know all things, in time and space, out of time and space, subsist within the One of Light, for love of **Truth**."*

Vinicius moves through the throng of people as we wait for Blessed Soup. I leave the line to ask for a translation of what the white slips of paper note. He announces that John of God prescribed herbs for both kids. This presents me with another dilemma. I am not going to purchase herbs knowing that their mothers will scoff at the thought.

Vinicius tells me to write the kids names, ages, and locations on the back of the pictures and deposit them into the basket as an alternative. I quickly do so, still confused and distraught, before getting back into the soup line.

A young man moves past me with bowls of Blessed Soup. He deposits them in front of an older couple already sitting at the corner table. One of them sits in a wheelchair. Minutes later the young man weaves through the row of tables with two more bowls of soup. He places one in front of an elderly man sitting with the couple and looks up at the crowd waiting in line. I feel very privileged as he motions me forward to sit and consume the soup. A large chunk of freshly baked white bread accompanies the soup. It's an end piece, my favorite.

*"Living in a state of grace is not as difficult as some might expect. It is a matter of tapping into the one of **All That Is**, which resides inside each living thing. To do this is as easy as stopping the flow of information coming in from outside sources. For humanity is but a vessel for*

All That Is *to work though and acknowledge the greatness therein.*

"*As you tap into this source of One know that all things come easily now. The veil of illusion lifts further as all regard themselves as one, holy BEing in a state of grace. Seek nothing outside this wondrous state of BEingness as old systems of earth continue to frail and fall by the wayside. There is nothing to stop humanity from reaching new and more life-affirming probabilities as all hearken to the Voice within.*

"*From this very state comes the knowing that humanity cannot fail in whatever it chooses to do henceforth.*"

What a joy it is to have like-minded friends! Faye and I discuss energies within the Current Room minutes later while sitting outside the Pousada. She informs me that Brazilians love their fireworks and shoot them off day or night. It explains the frequent sounds filling air space outside of Abadiania. Before we part, Faye reminds me to ask for ease and grace when transmuting discarnate energy. It will help greatly to ease the pain.

The blazing sun beckons me to snap a photo as I walk toward the Casa. Digital photos reveal another representation of Mother Mary. My digital camera then allows me to snap a few photos of the Italian invocation and statue of Our Lady of Montenero to compare with those taken at night. A beautiful, orange butterfly captures attention after purchasing more water that is blessed. It soars through the air, flirting with me, while I sense its true nature. The butterfly grants my request to float slowly, directly in front of me, for a photo. Life is amazingly good as I head back to the Pousada for lunch.

Continued Blessings

Tour group members welcome me upon entering the dining area. Someone places another chair at the full table so I can sit. Friendly conversation and good food make all the difference. Lunch is just as delicious as yesterday even though it's almost exactly the same kind of food. I'm still not tired of eating rice and beans twice a day. Today, kitchen workers present small pieces of chicken swimming in some kind of homemade tomato sauce. There's no need for a knife to cut fresh, organic vegetables down to size. It must take, I believe, a long time to prepare.

Everyone readily shares Casa experiences as we sit watching Faye look for cats in the nearby garden. Maria reminds us that many people seem to stay in Abadiania for extended periods. I ponder the thought once again. Two suitcases of clothes and other things are really more than enough, and I know, in the deep recesses of my being, I packed them just in case I decided to stay.

Napping after lunch is easy to do. But not hearing the usual messages from my Higher Self upon waking is a bit disheartening. I have been here for almost six full days and still have not recorded any messages or written. And I am not consciously drawing Light into my body as usual either. Perhaps it's part of the process.

The clock notes it's almost two o'clock when I rise for the short walk to see John of God. There's hardly anyone in the bookstore as I take a Second Time Line ticket, from a box on the counter near the door. I don't know a ticket is unnecessary. Those asked to return at two o'clock in the afternoon, or in the morning at eight, move through a different line.

Once again, I worm my way to the concrete bench at the side of the room. A man rises to offer his seat upon a blue chair as I begin to squirm behind the last row of chairs. People ready to have operations form a line quickly as I sit filling the air with Love and Light. Other Lightworkers are easy to spot when I open my eyes periodically. They too are spreading Divine Light.

"Every action serves a purpose. One must ask themselves: 'What purpose does this serve?' when acting under any circumstance. 'Whom do I serve? Do I serve only myself with this action or is it designed to serve the greater good?' Those actions serving the greater good will remain most welcome in the New World. Those actions meant to make one happy, fulfilled, or at peace serve the greater good.

"The farthest reaches of humanity now beckon forth a new age of love, peace, and understanding. Unity abounds within this new race of humans as we go forward into 2013. All come now knowing the Truth of ages that ye are free of yesterday's burdens.

"Seeking nothing but the love of Oneness, all humanity moves forward on this day of birth, your 12/21/12. Hearing nothing but the sweet sounds of unity brings one forth into greater evolution for all mankind."

Continued Blessings

In what seems like merely a few minutes, a speaker announces the 2:00 PM line. I rise to weed through the throng of people waiting on the right side. The friendly, Brazilian monitor quizzes me as I move into the line while trying to hand her my ticket.

"You are asked to return at 2:00 PM?" she asks.

I know she counted my hand when it rose after the speaker asked for people here for the Second Time Line.

"Yes," I reply while moving forward.

She takes my ticket without reply and continues to monitor the procession.

This line seems to move much more quickly than other lines. Perhaps, it's due to the smaller number of people in the procession. Vinicius moves toward me as I near John of God.

"The entity asked you to return at 2:00 PM?" he asks innocently.

"Yes. Don't you remember?"

"Sometimes I do not remember," he announces with a handsome grin as we move quickly before John of God. "There is a different entity this afternoon."

John of God scribbles on a small slip of white paper and thrusts if into my hand before waving me away.

I look at Vinicius with a questioning look.

"It is for your herbs," he says softly before turning to the next person in line.

A young woman quickly whisks me toward the Blessing Room. Today's blessing is easy to understand for the speaker says it in different languages. This time I don't cry but sense emotions rise as he speaks. I'm not sure of the need for Casa herbs. After years of taking handfuls of medications and supplements each day, I have weaned my daily practice down to three supplements. My habitual practice includes a morning antioxidant capsule and time-released B-complex and then fatty acids in the afternoon and evening. Sometimes I think even that is too many pills to take.

Bright sunshine greets those of us with paper slips as we head toward the Pharmacy to fill herbal prescriptions. The woman behind the counter offers me a large bottle of passion flower capsules with directions to take them three times a day. It costs an unbelievable $50.

I'm barely concerned with rules to follow while taking the herbs. Avoiding alcohol is no big deal. There are five bottles of good beer from Christmas 2009 still in my refrigerator and almost a full bottle of good wine used for cooking last year because I very rarely drink. I do not eat spicy peppers but will miss the taste of good pork. Only the thought of taking more pills bothers me as I walk back to the room.

Energies surround me much sooner upon lying down to nap after taking the first herb capsule. Flashes of light fill closed eye vision. I rise, feeling happier and lighter but there's still some right hip pain.

Two members of our group remain in their rooms after having surgery Friday afternoon. Faye reminds me again at dinner that we have to take this body along with us. This time we are not leaving an imperfect body behind but perfecting the one we have as we rid our soul of discarnate energy, to die while still in a living, human form. She verifies that the pain I feel so strongly now is old, deep-rooted, soul stuff surfacing to transmute.

I am still not sure about moving through the line when it begins again.

Continued Blessings

"*Choose your state of consciousness carefully and know that all states exist. You are reaching toward the Oneness of BEing on earth, something never achieved on any planet. As each reaches for its own state of BEing on this Earth Mother know that your state of consciousness carries you forward to the nirvana you seek in all aspects.*

"*Taking nothing for granted will carry you to the state of BEing you wish to exist in. We are now coming to one of the most opportune times in America's history. All lies in readiness to reach never before states of BEing, for humanity, as America's systems crumble. These old ways of greed and manipulation have no place in the New Earth. And so it is with great eagerness that we watch them crumble.*

"*You are alone in your own universe of thinking. What comes to you comes though your thoughts. This thought is possible through brain waves housed in your body and fed by every day occurrences. How you view the world changes with each day's events that you feed by thinking and paying attention to them. If you wish a better world in which to live you must guard your thoughts carefully, thinking only those life-affirming thoughts that you wish to feed. It is as simple as that. The more attention you pay to any subject, the more that subject, circumstance, increases in your world. As the ethers of earth continue to thin, this will become much more evident to those on earth.*"

"You are here for a reason," Faye announces. "Play by Casa rules."

That means going through the line and asking for help instead of just enjoying and adding to the wonderful streams of Light energy in current rooms. Although one receives healing while contributing to the energies, she notes, it is sometimes best to ask when we perceive a need.

Her words now make sense because everything is a game our souls chose to play. What a wonderfully, imaginative game this is, with so many people, so many ways to live, so many environments, conditions, and states of BEing! This is the game I choose to play and there's nothing to lose playing it by Casa rules.

"Things fall quickly into place as all realize the illusion of this earth game. Many now follow the path to Oneness knowing all here is but illusion. Keeping steady upon the path requires the constant letting go of old beliefs, thoughts, emotions, and circumstances that keep one only enmeshed in illusion. You must rely on your own small Self of One, to carry you toward true BEing, by honing its aspects to seek only the Higher Self of your being.

"Know that this period of time lasts but for a few months, for some. For others, not yet on the path, it has not begun. Each soul has its own journey to travel and yet all follow the path of masters. Seek ye not the Kingdom of God for it lies within."

Tonight I forego the trek to Café Central and slip into bed at 9:00 PM. I'm exhausted from lack of sleep and hoping to rest extensively during our four-day break. Sleep is again sporadic but there's more of it than previous nights. Small, creatures, which look like forms of silverfish, still bother me as they squirm on my bed during sleep.

Something wakes me between three and four o'clock in the morning. Casa entities are with me. I just know it. My yellow, smiley face light shines steadily as I take two pictures of white walls nearby. Digital photos show a blend of rainbow colors.

Blue, orange, gold, yellow and green colors on the wall

Chapter Four

Shades of Dilemma

We are all one family in the consciousness of light whether we are talking with angels, masters, elves or a mosquito. To enter, the web of Christ Consciousness asks us to dismantle the hierarchical systems, which belong only to the limited three-D world.
Dr. Christine Page - Spiritual Alchemy

Body pain is down to a minimum upon waking after 8:00 AM on Saturday. I'm on my own to eat a solitary breakfast before walking to the Casa with a camera. Much fewer people roam Casa grounds today. Pictures of the sun reveal Mother Mary's loving energy. Within the hour, I'm back in my room to check email and post photos on Facebook.

    A short walk to the hill with Cathy invigorates me before lunch. The area is a blend of dry weeds scattered upon red or brown earth, healthy looking trees, and tall green grass. We take pictures of the landscape and stare in awe as a butterfly obeys my request to let me photograph it. Rich, orange earth makes it difficult to spot the still brown, orange, and black butterfly, as it poses, but I take several pictures anyway.

    Statues sitting two yards from my Pousada door look blurry after our usual lunch. Opting to nap, I return to my room. Casa energies make themselves known minutes later. Five pictures taken in sequence show rainbow colored walls in my room. I rise quickly to see if new photos will reveal Casa energies within the statues sitting near my Pousada door. The statues appear normal.

Maria, Ernie, and I venture down to take pictures of the Casa and field across from it after dinner. Anxious to see if more orbs appear in photos, I walk slowly through the large, stark area asking for energies to show up. Many photos reveal jagged flashes of red or white light while others hold white, red or blue orbs. Some photos reveal both orbs and flashes of light. Various photos of Our Lady of Montenero again reveal a golden halo of light above the statues head. In these photos, the mist flowing below it, within golden waves of energy, is pink and blue.

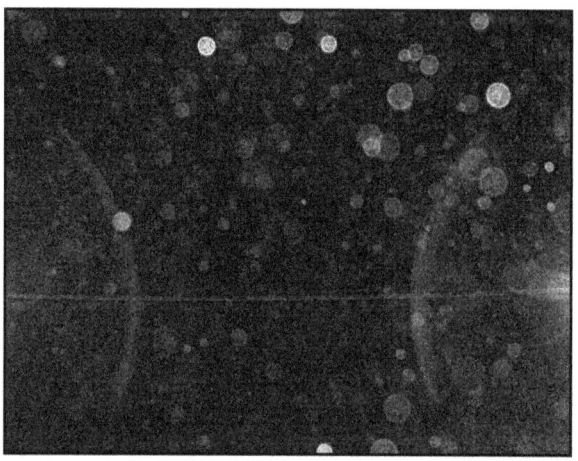

Spirit energies in a field across from the Casa

The full moon shines brightly on our way to Café Central. Fireworks sound in the distance as a large, dirty, white horse offers more photo opportunities. Orbs and flashes of red light appear. The crowd sits snapping shots of the horse while waiting for dandelion coffee. Two pictures of uniquely painted walls fascinate me. They capture the essences of Grainne and Joao quite well. Both are jovial, entertaining, and insightful people that juggle work and spirituality into the perfect blend.

The essence of Joao at Café Central

"I shall enjoy my hot shower this evening," I announce to the group before returning to the room, "if only in my mind."

"Good luck with that," they chorus still trying to figure out how to work the showerhead as well.

A slow stream of water from the shower comes out almost hotter than I can bear minutes later. I've solved the mystery! All it takes is a willingness to choose between a strong stream and hot water.

Sunday morning's breakfast crowd is much quieter than usual. Sporadic chatter seeps into my room until I rise right before the kitchen closes. It's nearly nine o'clock in the morning as I place fresh fruit and cheese upon a plate. Today's gift is the last of a loaf of whole grain bread. I place slices of cheese between heels of bread and put it into the sandwich maker. A worker slides past me seconds later to plug the appliance in with a smile.

    Sporadic thoughts keep me company while eating. Most members in the tour group have moved through Casa lines several times already. More than half experienced "spiritual interventions," by way of "psychic surgery" and some have had two of those. I appear to be the exception to the rule. Am I missing something?

    "Having a mind in a human body stops many from hearing the Voice within. This Voice is easily tapped when one clears the way by assuring that its physical host takes the time to hear. Not everyone will wish to hear messages from their Higher Self. But for those that do, the way to do so becomes easier when ones body is nurtured, and cared for, with the utmost respect.

    "Imbibing in detrimental substances such as tobacco, alcohol, and foods made by genetic manipulation stops the flow of Higher Self from coming though so easily. Assure that your physical host receives the needed sleep required for that too is another way that Spirit comes through the veil of illusion. Keep your physical host free of negative influence and steer clear of situations that may cause undue stress.

    *"We are aware that many more live in situations placing them in less than desirable conditions. But the small mind of one can be controlled easily, by the physical host, when it is clear of negative influence. Recall promptly that your thoughts manifest quickly to create your world. Concentrate only on life-affirming thoughts to tap into the Source of **All That Is**. For many that Source remains their Higher Self. For others it will be aspects of the soul, long forgotten. And for the very few who abide by all manifestations of Spirit, **All That Is***

comes through, rather easily, using the higher realms of illusory existence.

"Take the time to tap into this Source that flows readily each day. Know that another cannot control your mind unless you allow it to be so. Steer clear of mainstream media and other sources that strive to keep humanity in the throes of survival. And know, you are never, and shall never be alone in your efforts. The company of what you refer to as Heaven goes before you to pave the way to freedom."

The young man who sat with us at dinner the other night rolls his wheelchair into the dining area. We chat for several minutes. He's visited the Casa for many years and is surprised that I have not yet had "psychic surgery." Everyone, he notes, with a shrug and wide smile, has at least one while here.

"Surrender to the Casa rules," he announces before wheeling himself away.

A cat roams in the garden as I ponder his words. Why do I still not feel inclined to play this game? Is it because of the strong masculine energies or refusal to play by another's rules? Am I really relinquishing my power by playing this game or is it just a matter of changing perception to view things differently?

Sun shines brightly as I take more photos in front of the Pousada minutes later. Brightly colored orbs again offer a representation of Mother Mary. A wormhole appears to sit among blue, pink, and white orbs. I smile and move down the road to take my daily walk. Being here, and able to walk outside in this lovely weather, fills me with immense joy. On the way back to the Pousada, I stop to photograph a meaningful sign in the field across from the Casa.

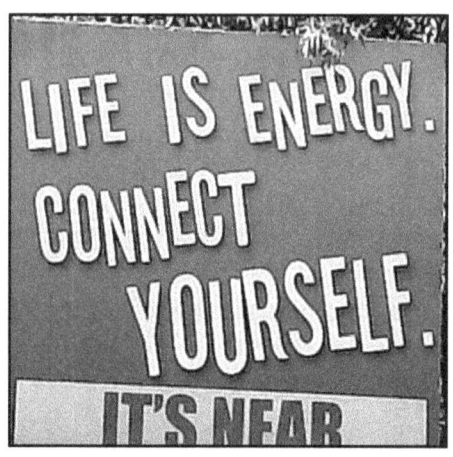

"Life is Energy, Connect Yourself. It's Near."

Yes! Everything is energy, all formed to create unique worlds. We reside in a world made with our own thoughts. No two worlds are the same. It is why we come here to play.

Faye finds me sitting outside the Pousada minutes later. Of course, we both know she's there by Divine Intervention. We soon stroll toward a small infrequently used café blocks away.

"It's best to fully surrender to Casa energies," she announces, as I voice apprehension over going though the line again. "We're playing a game and this is the game you chose to play or you wouldn't be here."

We talk for almost an hour while sitting beside a large, beautiful, swimming pool complimented by an expansive view of green, rolling hills. Faye offers valuable advice as I gaze at chickens, cows, and horses grazing in fields below us.

"Write down your concerns in detail and place them in the Casa's triangle. And then, buy yourself a small, wooden triangle and see what happens when you place it on your forehead to rest," she announces before we part.

I decide to follow Faye's advice. But even though there is something odd about the vision in my right eye, I ask only to heal discarnate energies within my soul as I scribble news of my dilemma onto a piece of paper.

Minutes after we part, I walk toward the Casa to place concerns into the large, wooden triangle hanging upon the waiting room wall. The bookstore is nearly empty when I enter to purchase a smaller triangle. The shopkeeper hands me several triangles. I am to decide which one is best and promptly choose one that appears more original. The wood holds more character and the triangle appears unique as opposed to some that look very similar.

Several members of my tour group sit eating lunch with others as I store the wooden triangle in my room. They pull up another chair to the full table as I walk toward food. This is such a friendly place with so many people, to share experiences with, that I have no problem speaking my mind today. All eyes are upon me while voicing my resolved dilemma. I'll move though the line again. And I'll ask for something. Maria surprises me by wondering out loud if she should stay for an extended time.

Connecting with Casa energies more fully sure sounds promising as I lie down to nap. The small, wooden triangle sits upon my forehead after waking. A soothing force field, similar to one that greets me at night, fills the room. Familiar, yet different, energies surround me.

After mentally agreeing to surrender to Casa energies, I let the entities know I'll play by their rules. Since they are on the astral level, they just may be more enlightened than I am. The bridge they offer is much appreciated but I will not do anything against the wishes of Higher Self. And I will keep in mind that even though masters may be more enlightened, they're just as much of an illusion in this game as I am.

"One can always seek out the words of wisdom from those illusory masters that dwell beyond the veil of time. These masters await the timing of your every wish and desire, even knowing those wishes and desires stem from a human brain within a small mind of one. It's not so much that they (the masters) have unknown wisdom to impart but that the teachings they impart remind you of what you already know. You are loved immeasurably and always watched over very carefully.

"All eyes are upon those on earth as humanity ventures through unknown territory. Humanity now breaks the distance of space and time by treading new waters to dwell in the Mind of One forevermore. Some may not consider this feat possible but we know it is accomplished already in other realms of time and space. The time/space continuum you appear to dwell in is but one of many areas not yet fully in Truth of Oneness. This shall be remedied soon as all come forth to feel the power of belonging to a group moving toward the wholeness of **All That Is***.*

"Many remain unaware of the struggle between light and dark that seems to continue full speed ahead on your planet. We speak for those not yet ready to acknowledge that there is no separation. It is only in time/space that this illusion exists. And yet, humanity feeds on this illusion and has for quite some time. The illusion will end as all come together after learning of falsities thrust upon them knowingly by those forgetting their True Self.

Shades of Dilemma

"*All aspects of the One must coalesce without differentiation of beliefs. This feat accomplishes much in other worlds as well, for many realms of illusion are now operating within those not yet ready to let go of the separation dream. Aspects of separation will be played out in other realms, as well as earth, until the time for all to meld arrives. This time creeps closer at an ever-quickening pace but consciousness continues to play a hefty role for now.*

"*The consciousness of humanity changes immeasurably at year's end. And dare we say, we being those on the other side of the illusion, that this consciousness stands to gain much through the rest of your year of trials and tribulations. Many people on your planet have lived through their trials and tribulations. You will find them in safe harbors holding the Light to lead all back to the Oneness of BEing. They are not saviors in any sense but aspects of yourselves now ready to return to the Wholeness left, if only in mind, many eons ago. All must come together for this feat to occur for it is all or none as noted throughout the ages.*"

Everyone in our group eats dinner late and moves down the road to Café Central. Tonight overpowering, stank odors of animal waste accompany us past the lone, skinny horse, dogs, and chickens. Many cats, dogs, horses, cows and chickens roam freely here and there does not appear to be any upkeep by the city. Thoughts of regular garbage pick-up and sanitation at home lull me into a minefield of separation while quickening the pace.

People fill the café beyond capacity. Some sit upon ledges near the street. Perfect timing helps us to snag a table as one empties. We soon fill it with jovial laughter and are the last ones to leave after 10:00 PM.

The skinny horse grazing near Café Central

    Our walk back to the Pousada again fills with a variety of unpleasant smells. The area is totally unlike my hometown where regulations require people who walk dogs to scoop up animal waste. I'm grateful for a small flashlight as we stroll. Thankfully, my room is now clear of any distasteful smells.

Chapter Five

Off to Pirenopolis

From a spiritual perspective, any and all physical assets and limitations are illusory, mere "life props." Yet a person's acceptance of or resistance to them is critical to entering spiritual adulthood. From a spiritual perspective, in fact, the entire physical world is nothing more than our classroom, but the challenge to each of us in this classroom is: Given your particular body, environment, and beliefs, will you make choices that enhance your spirit or those that drain your power into the physical illusion around you? Caroline Myss – Anatomy Of The Spirit

A large, luxurious bus arrives to chauffeur us to Pirenopolis after a late breakfast Monday morning. Vinicius is taking us to a waterfall but it involves lots of walking. Two people who had "psychic surgery" on Friday are not up to going. We pick up an additional passenger blocks away from the Pousada. The beautiful, Brazilian woman is cheerful and clearly full of Light.

There's plenty of room to stretch out on the bus as we travel down the tar-paved, two lane road. Vinicius is excited to show us what he says is the most beautiful part of Brazil. The landscape soon changes from a mix of red earth, dead grass, small bushes and trees to tall, green trees amid a lush display of rolling hills.

A Brazilian officer flags us down before we reach the city. Our driver spends several minutes showing him documents before we pass the checkpoint. The driver's music video plays on a small, television screen as we wait for approval. I'm dismayed to see it features the same codependence of many American songs. "When will people pay attention to words in songs?" I wonder.

"Ever-increasing energies continue to pummel the planet with new energies of Light. With each passing of the 'old guard' come clearer, cleaner energies, which make it possible for humanity to write a new script. This script far surpasses the old one where humanity left the planet not so gracefully.

"Keeping in line with these new energies is now the task of the forbearers, those in the forefront of massive change. Earth's forbearers are much different than in the past for they now carry the DNA of new life unknown on any planet or life system.

"The changes before humanity are now immensely progressing toward a new expansion of Wholeness, Beauty, and Love. This expansion is not seen on any other planet or system but unique for all life. The life that now blossoms is uniquely whole and filled with the substance of **All That Is**. Watch carefully in the days ahead as more of humanity come to know this Wholeness of Light and Truth.

"Your task is to assure that all know this is a natural course of events. It is a time where all humanity reaps the joy of Oneness. This true state is but a glimmer of hope and trust, a way to those wishing it forward. Thinking upon the Wholeness of **All That Is**, for all humanity to know, brings it ever closer.

"Great changes take place in the human body now. Sufficient rest is necessary along with the water you are accustomed to drinking during times of great thirst. Do not wait for this thirst but imbibe before it occurs to

Off to Pirenopolis

cleanse the body and keep it a clear channel. The body's needs continue to change as your DNA."

Sparsely planted small trees amid dry, brown earth divide streets as we move through town. After a sharp turn, we travel slowly down a narrow road made with what looks like very old, gray, clay bricks. Grass grows between the bricks. The area looks rundown but it's lined with cars on either side. At one point, a hefty driver moves to allow our bus to pass.

Another turn takes us down a wider street, with nicer looking houses, before we move back to a main road. Our big bus makes its way down a narrower, dirt road moments later as I marvel over the driver's skills. Dirt roads narrow yet again, as we make our way out of town. At times, I'm not sure we know the way. A white horse stands in the winding, dirt, country road as we wait patiently for it to move. Three more horses graze at the roadside yards ahead.

The bus soon stops to park under a shady tree. Chickens prance nearby as Vinicius speaks to the landowner. The Brazilian man requests the equivalent of $6.50 each to enter his property. He directs us to bathrooms and tells Vinicius how to reach the waterfall. We head toward outdoor restrooms to change into swimsuits.

A bevy of chickens gathers near one white and black rooster amid typical Brazilian squalor. They peck at pieces of waste, upon slabs of broken concrete, as the rooster peers into an empty, red pail. Propane tanks sit amid cleaning supplies and bags of waste hanging from a small tree.

LightworkersLog.com

A white and black rooster amid typical Brazilian squalor

The bathrooms, in my humble opinion, leave much to be desired as we head quickly back toward the bus after changing clothes. Vinicius directs us toward an old, wooden fence. Beyond the gate there appears to be some kind of fenced in area where animals may stay. There are no animals there now. We move ahead to walk through the smelly area toward a narrow dirt path, amid tall fields of grass. This is beautiful, energized country, and I sense it more as we step upon the path.

A black and white cow grazes in the field yards away from the path. Breathing labors as we move uphill so I slow down to catch my breath. I'm near the end of our procession. The young, Brazilian woman follows behind me until I tell her she is one of us and can move ahead. She seems right at home and accustomed to the altitude and exercise.

Our hike to the waterfall is much longer than expected. Monkeys cling to trees in the distance as we try to photograph them. Upon crossing a small stream, intuition guides me to touch the clear, cool water with my

Off to Pirenopolis

hand. I make the sign of the cross, by touching both sides of my chest and forehead, before moving ahead. It's not the first time something guides me to do so. Strange guidance for someone brought up as a Southern Baptist!

Our first glimpse of the waterfall shows a flowing stream of water cascading over what looks like black granite. The water looks magical up close. It seems surrounded by blue, heavenly mist while cascading down to a fairly, large pool of clear water.

Steve is first to plunge into the icy, cold stream. The young, Brazilian woman follows him minutes later. It takes me a while to enter and I stop moving when my pelvis gets wet. "This is far enough," I think, watching the others. "How do they get thoughts past the temperature so quickly?" It's hard enough to stay standing within frigid water. Steve continues to immerse his head under the steady stream as the Brazilian woman swims nearby.

The frigid waterfall

A beautiful, black butterfly, with seven yellow spots on each side, meets my request to be still while I photograph it before we leave.

Our walk back to the bus is quicker than to the waterfall. The Brazilian woman amazes me by making the trek in bare feet as I think about how dirty her feet will be. She reminds me it's a form of reflexology when I ask how she does it. Reflexology shoe inserts lie unused in a drawer back home after one use.

Vinicius directs the bus driver to a popular restaurant for lunch. The buffet is a welcome relief from our everyday fare back at the Pousada. I thoroughly enjoy it. Only chocolate is missing but, lo and below, individual packages of delicious truffles are for sale at the register!

An unexpected walk through town offers another opportunity for exercise and work. This is the most active I've been in quite some time. When we move slowly downhill, I hope there's no uphill climb later. Vinicius talks about the area, its history, and customs, as I lag behind. Because I live in the Present Moment, much of the time, history no longer interests me so I tone it all out. There's no longer a desire to dwell on the history of this illusion. Is it possible that thoughts allow it to exist? Could we spiral out of this world with joint thoughts of Heaven? If so, how many people would it take?

A one room police station and small park offer more photographic opportunities. Three people sit in chairs within the station, facing a single open window, as we pass before reaching a small parking lot with a motorcycle, two identical, older Volkswagens, and two newer small cars.

Off to Pirenopolis

The local swimming hole

The parks water looks inviting while we walk, beginning to sweat, along the road. Vinicius talks of more history to the small group later as I stand yards out of earshot. He then heads back to get the bus many blocks away.

Town history remains unknown to me as I listen to the wisdom of my soul. I'm guided to transmute negative energies after everyone exits an outside pavilion to sit in a garden-like area nearby. The beautiful Brazilian woman watches with curiosity as intuition leads.

Rituals such as this are not new to me when seeming to be 'on vacation.' I now stand in the middle of the pavilion and raise my arms. The town's negative energies transmute easily before filling the area with Light. When the task is complete, I sit beside the Brazilian woman who now is smiling widely.

"It's my secret job," I note with a shrug.

She nods her head in silence.

"The seeds of change are firmly in place since earth's Autumn Equinox. The lightbearers now move

forward to change the world in a new way. This is a new era that no one spoke of, or prophesized, for it is coming about as the seeds of change blossom through efforts of lightworkers throughout the world.

"Your time to blossom and go forth to spread the word of One creeps nearer with each thrust of earth's change. This is happening to all those who bear the Light of One willingly, and knowingly. You may not like the way these earth changes come about but make no mistake they are not occurring to assist any one member of earth's society. Each change completes an avenue for the many clans, or tribes, as some would call them, to complete eons of soul work not completed throughout the ages of time.

"The placement of each lightworker holds the grid's Light most securely. Each bearer of Light is secluded in their own space to complete their soul's work. You are but one of many thousands of lightbearers who now move forward to seal the deal. The deal of coming forward to secure earth's future in a new way, unheard of, unthought of, and unknown to all, until it occurs. Have no ill thoughts as you move forward to complete your task. Secure your future as a master lightbearer by moving forward and knowing that you hold the key to this New Earth. It is your new home to mold with your thoughts."

Our bus stops at another scenic waterfall on the way back to Abadiania. We walk slowly down a long set of steep, concrete stairs to reach toilets before climbing back up to the small outside café. I've had my fill of exercise and am ready to sit and rest. There's no what I refer to as "jello" here so I order Coke in a can and take my seat to photograph the expansive view.

Off to Pirenopolis

Two large waterfalls sit beyond an expanse of brown earth, weeds, green grass, and tall trees. A representation of Mother Mary again appears in pictures of the sun shining though a nearby tree. I'm still in a state of awe to see it for this phenomenon is new to me. After years of snapping shots of the sun, I have never seen this, except here in Brazil. My cheap camera does not take very good pictures but these photos are the exception.

Pink and golden spirit energies amid skies of blue

It really pays to have such a wonderful guide who gets permission to take us to places away from Abadiania. But exercising as much as we did today is not part of my usual routine. Worn out by the time we reach our Pousada, I move slowly to shower and sleep after dinner.

Casa entities make themselves known by blowing out the travel candle as I sleep. The candle refuses to stay lit even after I relight it. Bugs wake me in the wee hours of the night. They apparently don't know that this room is my sanctuary. After years of taking bugs outside, now irritated, I flick these off my body and stomp on them before returning to sleep.

Chapter Six

Surrender at Last

When we surrender, we then begin the new and perfect connections that the solstice energies came to deliver. Karen Bishop – *The Wearing Away Of Our Ego Selves And Connecting To Our Brothers And Sisters*

The triangle now replaces my usual morning practice of drawing Light into every space within the body. It sits upon my forehead, on this Tuesday after waking early, and within minutes, the familiar energy field surrounds me. My small tape recorder at bedside remains unused. I miss not getting the usual messages but don't even feel the need to record the trip. I've sporadically noted hints to help me recall things if necessary. My eyesight remains unchanged.

Yesterday's walking was more than I'm accustomed to. However, getting more exercise is a good thing. Joints ache but the pain is not enough to stop me from walking with Faye before lunch. Faye has taken it upon herself to feed stray cats near the Pousada. We head towards the grocery store less than a mile away so she can buy cat food. There are no such stores in the small town near the Casa.

Today we celebrate Winter Solstice, here in Brazil, knowing this powerful time affects our journey. We walk at a rather slow pace talking about Casa energies until reaching the busy highway. How amazing that every shop in town has the full approval of unseen entities, as noted by John of God. Many shop proprietors also volunteer at the Casa with some serving as monitors, guiding visitors within current rooms. It's a whole different world across the busy roadway.

Small, colorful shops with clothing and other merchandise line the other side of the thoroughfare. As we wait for traffic to pass before running across, I recall hearing that during the first visit we are not to cross this main road. These merchants may not participate in Casa activities as the ones near the Pousada and, I think, we are to concentrate solely on the simple things in life rather than spend our time shopping.

Since Vinicius is my tour guide, the group is blessed and able to do things usually not done on the first visit. I don't want to push my luck so I opt to return and nap. Faye makes her way across the busy street alone.

The wooden triangle sits upon my forehead minutes later. Tingling creeps across the top of my head while envisioning an opening crown chakra. Soul's deeply rooted, negative energies transmute easily, with help from Casa entities. Upon rising, neck stiffness accompanies ringing in the left ear. A bit of discomfort remains in finger joints and my right hip.

Crown chakra tingling occurs hours later while uploading pictures of the sun to Facebook. Photos taken while standing in the Casa's empty, meditation pavilion show different types of spirit energies. Various shades of pink orbs float below a spinning top, amid two golden orbs.

We meet Grainne later in the afternoon at the pizza place. She kindly agreed to tell us the story of how she and Joao got together. The tale is inspiring, funny, and very entertaining, especially the way Grainne tells it. Both she and Joao share the wonderful experience of basking in healing Casa energies.

Surrender at Last

Dinner later in the evening is the same with few variations in food preparation but I love it just the same. As family and friends back home, everyone I sit with tonight seems to speak of separation and personal matters. I feel distanced with a strong desire to speak only of unseen energies and ascension.

Vinicius is supportive later, when I mention the eyesight dilemma, but does not agree that asking for help is giving my power away. He nods his head in agreement when I opt to move though the line again. I choose not to name the disorder that seems to show up for it only feeds it energy. This time I will ask the entities for clear vision, a perfectly matched spiritual partner, and greater spirituality.

Although it may be hard to believe for some, everything is energy that we feed with the power of thought. Thoughts transform possibilities into physical reality. Every thought represents an electrical charge and cannot be without effects. Yes, absolutely everything has origin in thought. Thought waves circulate throughout space and the stronger the thought, the more people that believe in it, the quicker it manifests. When we fail to share a thought system, we weaken it.

We always experience the belief we project. Everything we think about affects our health, wealth, and happiness. It's important to know that thoughts control us unless we control our thoughts. Positive thoughts reap positive experiences. Changing beliefs form new patterns of thought. Changing ones mental attitude, to be more in harmony with ones true nature, always results in good, for Infinite Intelligence surrounds us and reacts to our thoughts. We more consciously create an enhanced life experience, by redirecting thoughts, turning to the power within to lift thoughts to union with Creation, which is perfect and complete. Collective positive thought now changes the world in ways like never before.

Wednesday dawns as most days in Abadiania at this time of year. Clear skies allow the sun to warm temperatures from the lower sixties to eighty degrees. My full, white skirt flows in the breeze as we make our way to the Casa after breakfast.

Many more people walk towards the Casa today. Everyone knows we will celebrate Joao's birthday in two days. Colorful balloons hang in various places throughout the beautiful grounds. More people than usual come from all over the world to bask in the energies and celebrate with fireworks, music, and free food. Several tour buses sit quietly in the usually empty field. Small cars fill the parking lot.

After entering through the side entrance, I stand with many others waiting to flow into lines. *Amazing Grace*, revised of course, rings through my brain as people repeat time-worn prayers about someone outside of themselves. I then switch to "Lightworker Mode," radiating Light and Love throughout the room.

The speaker announces "Operations." A woman nearby quickly rises to flow into the line so I can sit in her warm seat. Another speaker soon announces formation of the Revisions Line. I settle back into "Lightworker Mode" to tone everything else out.

Several minutes later, it's music to my ears upon hearing, "Second Time Line." The woman seated next to me immediately stands to let me out. A monitor quickly takes my ticket as the line moves forward.

Before long, Vinicius accepts the white slip of paper from my hands to remind him of my desires. The entity quickly announces, "Operation" and John of God focuses on the next person in line. Vinicius smiles knowingly as he translates the words into English. I am in a bit of shock as a young woman points me toward the Blessing Room.

Although I've avoided going to a doctor, or getting eyes checked for new glasses, the news that I may not be as perfect as envisioned comes as a surprise. There's no doubt that the afternoon's procedure will be psychic surgery and not the physical type like Ernie had when entities helped John of God to remove a large tumor from his spine years ago. My right eye begins to ache.

Vendors line the path back to my room. A smiling, dark-haired Brazilian wears a cap similar to mine and beckons me over to inspect her beautiful, handmade wares. She is, I note with surprise, the wonderful counter woman at the pizza place who goes into the back to get me "jello" for my Diet Coke with added Vitamin B. But I am no longer a consumer and continue to downsize. The last thing I need is more stuff to cart from here to there.

According to my camera, it's not quite nine o'clock in the morning when I reach the Pousada. I will stay sequestered, alone in my room, for twenty-four hours after surgery so the urge to stay there now is gone.

Sun shines into the camera lens minutes later as I hold it up to snap today's representation of Mother Mary. I just know she will be there. Two photos show white, pink, and golden yellow orbs coming from the sun. The essence of Mother Mary soars among them. I smile and move back to the Casa for more photos and water blessed by the entities. Water costs about the same as spring water back home and packs a powerful punch of healing energies.

LightworkersLog.com

White, pink, and golden yellow orbs coming from the sun

Several pictures of Mother Mary holding Jesus and Our Lady of Montenero fail to reveal anomalies. Pictures of crystals, held within the confines of a glass-enclosed case outside the bookstore, fill my Smart Card, so I turn the camera off before sitting on a wooden bench in the outside meditation pavilion.

Being in a small community of like-minded souls is very nurturing. Our group sits together for lunch as we discuss the morning's events. Everyone nods with wide smiles when I announce my upcoming surgery. Cathy knows the rules and immediately asks if I'd like her to bring me dinner. I'm grateful for the offer while heading to the pizza place for a Diet Coke with a bit of "jello."

People spill out of the Casa's main hall onto crowded walkways, and grounds, at 2:00 PM. A speaker announces someone's birthday. Another speaker stands nearby holding his hands together in somewhat of a triangle below his waist. The symbol reminds me of many times when I did the same, sometimes not realizing it, or knowing why. Is he grounding into Mother Earth using a

Surrender at Last

Diamond Mudra to direct energy? Is this something we learned from Lemuria?

Many stand among the sitting mass waiting to form lines while others mill about outside trying to get closer. After failing to find a seat, I stand amid wheelchairs on the side near the Current Room entrance.

A tall, young stranger stands pouring Light into the room while up against the wall with many others. He motions with his eyes before moving away and I gladly take his place. The speaker calls for those having operations minutes later.

Psychic surgery seems like an easy way to rid myself of an eye disorder. I enter the moving line easily as it flows toward John of God. The woman who owns a shop filled with fragrant oils, candles, lotion, and other merchandise leads the group meditating as I move through the first Current Room. John of God is not sitting in his chair as usual. In fact, I don't see him anywhere, which is not to say he is not there.

The swiftly flowing line continues to move until we reach the Blessing Room. A petite woman motions for us to sit on wooden benches, side-by-side as usual. Another man begins to repeat prayers while we sit with closed eyes. I'm not sure how many of us there are. But we fill the room and perhaps spaces in the room before as well. The other two members of my tour group, who were also scheduled for psychic surgery this afternoon, are nowhere in sight.

A prayer, at least I think that's what it is, continues to flow through the room. But since it's in another language, I do not understand the words. That is the extent of surgery. Someone hands me a white slip of paper before another woman directs me to wait for other surgical patients outside on a concrete bench in the shade.

Dark sunglasses cover eyes and now I'm wearing my hat, glad to remember Ernie's advice to protect the eye after surgery.

We listen intently as a woman notes the slip of paper in our hand is a prescription for herbs. Entities imbue individual prescriptions with unique energies for each patient. If the entities prescribed other herbs before now, we are to stop taking them until we finish these. We must act as if we really just had physical surgery. That means we must get our herbs before taking a taxi to our room to recuperate for twenty-four hours.

Someone will bring us the Blessed Soup tomorrow morning (after we sign up for it upon reaching our Pousada) and we are to sleep as much as possible. We must refrain from speaking to others and if we have not asked someone to bring our meals, remain silent while getting them before returning to our room. No reading, no electronics, I think the woman notes with authority.

My eyes, I know, must rest, especially the right one, which continues to ache as she talks. It feels as if an eye specialist scraped it. There's no doubt that something happened as I try to keep my right eye closed.

Entities will visit us, during the twenty-four hour period and in seven days, to remove "the stitches." We must write our name and the address we will be at, onto a slip of white paper and place it in the basket, before going to the onsite Pharmacy. We are also to refrain from exercise for seven days and, if leaving, must allow someone else to lift our luggage. There will be no eating of pork or spicy peppers, drinking alcohol, or sexual relations for the next forty days. We must follow the directions accompanying our herbal prescriptions as well.

I am one of the first to write my name and address on the white slip of paper. For me, it's a milestone because I rarely give out my home address. It just makes sense now to abide by Casa rules. After getting more herbs, I sit upon the concrete bench, near a long line of taxi's, waiting for the other two members of my tour group.

We soon nod to one another and pile into a small taxi for the two minute drive to the Pousada. The young, Brazilian, desk clerk smiles as we write names on the Blessed Soup Delivery List for tomorrow before heading alone to our rooms.

Extreme tiredness overwhelms me. It's surprising because last night I slept better than since my arrival and lately my energy level increased. I fall asleep easily after taking the new herbs but a knock on the door wakes me a few hours later.

Cathy's beautiful, smiling face greets me upon opening the door. She hands me a plate with salad and chicken and a small cup of rice and beans.

"I'll go get you some fruit," she announces turning back towards the door.

"Thank you," I reply absolutely thrilled, "this is more than enough."

"Do you want me to bring you breakfast before I go to the Casa tomorrow?"

"No, I can zip out of my room in the morning. I'll probably be bored by then."

"I know I was," she replies with a wide grin. "Do you want me to get you a Diet Coke with jello?"

"No, I can do without one today. Thanks."

"See you tomorrow afternoon then."

The meal is one of the best I've ever had as I eat with my right eye closed. When it's all gone, I realize the chicken was fried. I very rarely eat fried foods but love fried chicken.

Sleep quickly claims me again. Unseen forces surround me whenever I wake. The feeling is quite familiar. My right eye is still very sore. I keep it closed while awake. During the wee hours of the night, the entities come to work on me. I feel their presence in the room, around 4:00 AM, and fumble trying to grab the camera from the night stool to get a shot of the wall. The photo display shows slightly colored walls similar to rainbow pictures taken earlier in the week.

Hunger rouses me out of bed shortly after hearing the kitchen help open the doors. After donning my dark sunglasses, I am the first to fill my plate with fresh, organic fruit, cheese, and freshly baked cookies. Two people enter the area as I silently move back to my room. When the plate is empty, I return it to the kitchen without talking to anyone.

There's no need to write for the first time in years. The travel candle stays lit because my room is dark. Boredom fills me so I place headphones on to hear beautiful music. My eyes open when the CD ends. The candle goes out and then a light shines, glimmers, flashes once.

My brain hears something about "going home" and then, "Spread the news of the Casa. All is well. Do not fear in the days ahead. The days of woe are numbered."

"Ageless truths face humanity now resting in the innocence of beginning. This beginning is but a whisper away from new truths, as yet untold. All now reap the beginning of each process to further humanity's rest from that of gross innocence of BEing to full readiness to participate in the upper echelons pushed aside for eons of time.

"As you move into this process let all things old fall away for the time of new, much greater, awareness now beckons all toward the fullness of BEing. All those on the path before you applaud your efforts to forgo eons of misuse and abuse of power.

"Those not yet in line with the ageless Truth of **All That Is** will soon erupt into the grossness of new truths, where the awareness becomes undeniably known. This will move humanity forward as a whole, as those not ready to forgo the game of manipulation and power now leave this planet to play their game elsewhere.

"Your planet Earth is now quickly moving toward the wholeness of **All That Is**. We watch with great anticipation as those ready to step up to the plate, so to speak, do so to lead the others forward. It is with great pleasure that we guide those willing to the fullness of Self in all aspects.

"The days ahead may appear grossly unbalanced in many ways. But you must move forward in your thinking, knowing that all is indeed in Divine Order."

It's a good feeling to sense the force field and a good message to hear today. My eye still aches but I know all is exceedingly well as sleep claims me once again.

Hours later, a knock sounds on the door. It's the smiling desk clerk with a large bowl of Blessed Soup. An end piece of bread accompanies the soup. I so love the end piece of a loaf of bread!

When the soup is gone, I place the bowl outside on the metal table near my door, and surprisingly, fall back asleep for several minutes. I then begin to pack. In two days, we will be on our way towards the airport and since there's nothing else to do, it just makes sense to pack.

I finish packing most of my things after eating a light lunch. Shortly after three o'clock in the afternoon, a full twenty-four hours later, I head toward the pizza place to get my Diet Coke with "jello." Two photos of the sun delight me with their representations of Mother Mary.

Today I'm pleased to receive five pieces of ice instead of the usual three. Maria chances upon me as I suck on the last ice cube.

"I've been looking for you," she happily announces with a wide smile. "Would you like to share some Acai Pudding with me?"

"Sure," I announce after swallowing the ice, "why not? I'm happy to see you too Maria."

She quickly orders two bowls of Acai Pudding. It's soon clear that Maria has decided to stay, even if she doesn't quite know it herself. I too sense the entities asking me to remain but am not inclined to do so. My unique work must take place in the U.S. But I am prepared to leave a sizable donation to John of God and write about this trip. I don't share the revelation with Maria as she continues to share feelings.

We chat for several minutes while eating the freshly made, delicious pudding. Words flow out of my mouth but I have no idea what they are shortly after they reach her ears. All I know is that Maria will stay to bask in healing Casa energies after our tour group leaves.

Vinicius sits in the dining room right after they open the kitchen doors. He kindly agrees to hear about my experience and plans. Tomorrow morning, I will move through the Second Time Line again to ask for a blessing. I want to tell everyone of my Casa experience through a book. The Goodbye Line will carry me to John of God during the afternoon session.

A part of me feels it must contribute to this venture in a big way in order to leave. My wonderful guide looks surprised when I offer him a huge birthday gift for Joao and a much smaller one for himself. Our tour includes a generous Casa donation and money for his services but I'm compelled to give gifts anyway. In my mind, it will be well worth it to have clear vision without going through the hassle of a 'sick-care system' or experiencing physical surgery.

Everyone sits together for dinner later. We share experiences with a great deal of exuberance. All eyes are upon me as I announce my right eye still hurts. Although I never have, so I don't know what it really feels like, it still feels like I had physical eye surgery.

A few of us continue the conversation at Café Central after dinner where Grainne gives us a hearty hug. The white horse strolls by as we talk. Our evening is complete after drinking dandelion coffee, complimented by a chocolate chip cookie, a gift from Cathy. What a wonderful way to spend time, with good food, in the company of friends, and immersed in healing Casa energies!

Fireworks fill the air around four o'clock in the morning. My room is dark. The second set of batteries no longer shines the portable, smiley face light. A car equipped with intrusive loudspeakers drives by the Pousada very slowly. Traffic has definitely increased and I know it's due to today's celebration. Flashes of light, seemingly within my right eye, let me know there are energies at work.

Consciousness resides in everything. Jagged flashes of white light continue to appear both day and night. In time, I'll know these blessings are many beings of Light, of various intensities, gracing me with their presence. These darting sparks of love and consciousness, weaving in and out of reality, always bless with love. The constant reminders note, I'm not alone on this journey of awareness, for others exist within that invisible tapestry in which we live.

Dawn breaks on Friday morning to find my vision seems to remain the same. My right eye is still sore but faith sustains me. Dis-ease heals on the astral level first so there's no need for concern. Everything manifests first there. It always takes some time to become apparent here because we chose to forget our true nature to play the game of limitation on earth.

There is always a reason for dis-ease. The physical body allows Consciousness to function on earth and is merely a learning tool for the Mind. What I see is an effect brought about by thought, ideas, and beliefs. For years, I did not wish to see the world in which I live or even want to be here. Now I believe dis-ease keeps me more mired in this illusory world so it's only a matter of time before this oddity disappears. I AM, and always have been, perfect, whole and complete, one with *All That Is*.

"*Morphing physicality of the human form continues. Let all know that this is a natural course of events as bodies move closer in tune to the vibrational nature of Mother Earth. All things are not as they seem as bodies withstand these changing atmospheric pressures at a greater pace than ever before. Let all know that these changes are wholesome to the body, despite medical authorities' attempts to quell their occurrence by manipulating the human form.*

"Your earth changes to match more clearly the vibration it left many, many eons ago. As all upon her continue to morph as well there will be many who remain unable to withstand these physicality changes. Of course, they will be afforded another opportunity, if desired, to match these frequencies, with ease, upon newly formed human bodies through rebirth on earth.

"Your sun plays a major role in these coming and ongoing changes. Many, who attempt unsuccessfully to stem the natural flow of events towards full BEingness for all upon Mother Earth, know this. These attempts are feeble, at best, but do have some effect on humans not ready to face a morphing physicality with grace and ease. As these humans leave your planet, those new souls coming in will assure that earth's vibration matches their own with ease and grace."

Today is the busiest day of the year at the Casa because it is the day of Joao's birth. If they did not come earlier this week, the other people ready to celebrate will be here today. Gratitude fills me upon knowing that I will not be sitting in the current rooms for the sessions are likely to be much longer than usual.

We leave fifteen minutes earlier to reach the Casa. There are many more people walking with us. Today, we follow the procession slowly, like trained sheep following a Shepard, rather than weave though the stream.

"They're going to call the Second Time Line right after operations," I announce, while skirting around a pile of horse dung.

"How do you know?" someone asks.

"Because I am in that line and won't have to wait today."

"Well, it will be interesting to see what occurs," a tall man announces before entering Casa grounds.

Smiling, I continue silently repeating, "Second Time Line called second," while walking quickly toward the bookstore for a ticket. After several days of watching and listening, I now know there are seven possible lines that weave from the waiting room through current rooms to see John of God. The operations, revisions, eight o'clock and two o'clock lines appear shorter than the first or second time lines. This afternoon's Goodbye Line, I surmise, will be longer than usual.

A blonde-haired, French Canadian woman stands to allow me entry, to the concrete bench, after squeezing my way through the dense crowd. I am still silently repeating, "Second Time Line called second." She stands amused as the woman in front of her dunks down so I can swing both legs over her head to place knees between seats. Thank God, I'm wearing long, white pants today. There's literally no space between the last row of blue seats and concrete bench where I now rest feeling like a canned sardine.

The speaker announces "Operations" as I sit with palms facing up upon my thighs with eyes closed. Although difficult to do, I continue to fill the room with Light and Love. Minutes later, the same speaker announces formation of the "Second Time Line."

The French Canadian woman stands quickly to let me out. But the one in front must duck her head so I can raise both legs over it to get out. They applaud when I do so with little effort. Yes, I am in the flow of positivity and gratefulness!

After several days of watching lines form and move, I know the exact course to get me quickly into the line. People massed together seem to part as I approach to slide into the flowing procession. A monitor takes my ticket with a smile as the line continues to draw me closer to the entities.

Vinicius nods and smiles as I approach John of God. I quickly remind him of the desire for a blessing to write about my Casa experience. Before the words flow out of his mouth, John of God reaches his left palm out towards me. Stunned with surprise, I slowly place my right palm in his as Vinicius words cease. John of God smiles and delivers a brief response in Portuguese as Vinicius quickly translates. The entities have given me their blessing to write about my Casa adventure. I'm ecstatic.

More vendors, with a variety of wares, line the road to garner attention as I make my way back to the Pousada. The small, wooden triangle sits upon my forehead after lunch while lying on the thin mattress. Immense energies surround me, and just as at home, heat pours out from the center of my heart to warm my entire body. It's not as uncomfortable as usual because today's weather is much more comfy. One with *It*, I allow the energies to do their work. Sleep claims me when the energies dissipate.

Maria and Ernie stroll ahead of me, down the small street towards the sound of music, after I wake. My pace quickens to reach them seconds later in front of a nearby Pousada. They're in deep conversation, about the possibility of staying longer than expected, so I move on.

Later in the afternoon, it seems useless to wander and look for a seat after entering the side entrance of the Casa with triangle in hand. There are just too many people. I stand, as if packed in a community of identical sheep, near the Current Room entrance. Many people hold flowers, triangles, crystals, and other things. They will join me in the Goodbye Line; it's a sure bet.

Blessings cascade down from above as the speaker calls for "Operations." Today, he announces with a grin, anyone can spontaneously enter the line for an operation. And, wonder of all wonders, you get the special dispensation of still being allowed to attend tonight's party! Pandemonium fleetingly fills the room. A mass of excited people merge swiftly into the long line.

Several minutes later, the speaker announces "Goodbye Line."

I walk briskly through current rooms. Intense energies cloak everything and everyone with loving, purifying, cleansing Light. It's a wonderful place to be. There is absolutely no doubt that I could stay among this group of humans, to merge with Casa entities three days a week. However, my soul-given task back home is not complete. Even if it were, why would I wish to live in a country where most people live under what I now refer to as limiting conditions? Part of my soul journey, I strongly believe, is to rise from rags to riches and I will continue to do so showing everyone the Power of *All That Is* within human form. There is no need to live in limitation. And yet, could I not complete my task here? Could I not change my perception of limitation? It is a heady thought!

The procession moves much faster this afternoon. John of God scribbles upon my triangle before immediately responding to the next person in line. It looks like he has graded me with an A-!

Steve announces that we'll try to get a group photo with John of God when the session ends. A musician sings softly into a microphone at the nearby Pousada as I pass on the way to get a camera.

Unseen energies make themselves known through photos of Our Lady of Montenero. Another sequence of pictures, taken while standing in the meditation pavilion, shows what appears to be Mother Mary emerging from bright, afternoon sun. Several lines must still file past John of God so I leave Casa grounds to drink my last Diet Coke at the pizza place.

It's nearly six o'clock in the evening and we are still waiting to see if John of God will allow pictures today. "Since this is not our true form," I think, "and he is not the one who does the work he will not. Why would he wish, in this time of mass enlightenment, to pacify ego into believing it is real? Furthermore, why would I disregard my recently new practice of not photographing human forms?"

I leave the dwindling group of fans and groupies to eat an early dinner. Very few people sit in the dining area tonight and none of their energies draws me to join them. A lone woman asks to sit with me halfway though the meal. Like-minded energy attracts the same. There are no exceptions.

We immediately begin a long, treasured conversation about our true selves. Humans are parts of *All That Is* living in a Matrix of unlimited possibilities. Infinite Intelligence surrounds us and reacts to our thought. Although *All That Is* permeates everything, this world, this earth, and everything we see, is part of a game, an illusion that is not a part of what many refer to as God. The earth game is only one of many, many, other games played on an infinite number of planes. The game endpoint is when we all realize we are part of One and unify in Love.

My new friend is soon trying to wrap her mind around the reality that we are verifying one another's thoughts. Surprisingly, we grew up in the same state and now reside in Florida, hours away from each other! I assure her, that's the way it works when you're in the flow. People, suddenly and quite unexpectedly, come into your life to answer timeworn questions.

Members of my tour group dwindle in to join the table as she rises to leave. This is our last dinner together and now it's almost time for the kitchen to close. Two people behind the kitchen counter agree to keep doors open until the others arrive. They are still at the Casa with many more people because they served to enhance Casa energies in the Current Room this afternoon.

Maria announces her decision to stay when everyone finally sits together. We all commend her courage to face the unknown alone. Staying beyond the two-week tour, I assure her, will offer a plethora of new opportunities to think out of the box and enrich her life immensely.

Fireworks with orbs to celebrate Joao's birth

Fireworks fill the sky moments after we rise from the table. The street fills with people and many quickly move toward the celebration. Maria, Ernie, and I watch

Surrender at Last

beautiful fireworks from the front of our Pousada before strolling down to join them.

Music sounds throughout the small town of Abadiania as we approach the party. Banners congratulating Joao on his seventieth birthday line the fence. An undeniable wave of excitement fills the air. Smiling, very happy people, mill about the field. There are so many people that it's hard to get around. Upon sensing unseen energies, I wonder if some of those before me are forms visiting from the ethereal world.

Fire seems to replace body parts in photos

A bizarre scene meets my eyes. Many people dance or watch the band play as others stare in wonder at the billowing fire. Photos show transparent fields of energy. Body parts are missing as fire shows up in photos to replace them. Wisps of mist flow from many in the crowd. Unseen energies fill me with liveliness as I snap

LightworkersLog.com

photo after photo of the musicians on stage. There has never, to my recollection, been a time when I've felt so alive with this kind of awesome energy.

Orbs and usually unseen energy fill the field

Spirit energies appear in every photo amazing Maria and Ernie. Some usually unseen forms of energy completely cover body parts of people nearby. Orbs of various colors fill the air and now, looking at the crowd, I again wonder if everyone here is really someone in a 'government documented' physical body. Can they, if approached, reveal documents to verify their birth on this planet? Or have the unseen come to celebrate as well?

The jury is out as I continue to snap photo after photo. I only know that this is the best I have felt in many, many years. It's enough to make me change my mind to stay for I could definitely live forever basking in these energies.

Surrender at Last

John of God passes quickly through the crowd and out into the street as we continue to enjoy the scene. People stand with wide, open mouths as he weaves past. Grainne joins us for a photo opportunity before we merge into the food line. It is a very long, slow moving line.

More spirit energies grace the scene

I watch people's energies merge in photos on the camera's display as we patiently wait to advance in line. The line does not seem to move at all. Maria and Ernie hold my place when I move out of it to take more photos. A close view of the seating area shows tables full of people enjoying free food. No wonder the line is not moving, there's no room for more people in the large area. Several, huge, white layer cakes sit upon tables lined up against the wall.

LightworkersLog.com

Fire again seems to replace body parts as energies soar

We decide to leave by the time I rejoin Maria and Ernie. It will take another hour to enter the food tent based on how slow the line moves now. Our tour bus will arrive early on Saturday morning and I want to get some sleep. Totally energized within these energies, I dance my way off the field before calling it a night.

Chapter Seven

Blessings Abound

The promptings of the Spirit are revealed as Inner Teacher and Guide in direct proportion to the degree to which we learn to manage our conscious mind activity.
Helen Brungardt-Pope – For the Aspiring Mystic

Something prompts me awake near midnight. I reach out to the small, brown, wooden footstool nearby, which holds a little, green lamp. Eyes rest on a looming figure upon the floor. A large, brown, hairy spider sits near the single bedpost less than a foot away. It's about the size of my small palm. Intuition says it's a tarantula.

Are their bites poisonous?

Unpleasant thoughts of Brazilian hospitals rule as my heart quickens. "It's a test," my brain announces with a laugh. "Remember when you sat next to Steve and Cathy, at different times, and prompted them not to panic over a bee? Although they voiced apprehension about being allergic, as the bee flew increasingly closer, you told them it was a test. And they passed with flying colors. This, my dear, is your test."

Dumbfounded, I sit up, wondering what to do. There's a sense that this tarantula is harmless and here to deliver a message of great significance. And yet, my brain runs through all the possibilities.

How long has it been here? How did it get in? Did it crawl through the wide gap under my door or skirt in when I opened it tonight? Has it been under that bed for the past two weeks sustaining it's self on ants and other small creatures that creep under the door? Or, wonder of all wonders, did it just appear out of thin air like other creatures and anomalies I see?

It's not like I can call a desk clerk. There are no phones in our rooms and no one, to my knowledge, staffs the front desk after 11:00 PM, unless of course they expect previously booked guests to arrive. And there are no arrivals tonight for the Pousada is at full capacity.

Should I rise and ask to share a bed with either Cathy or Steve who are rooming on either side of me? Or should I handle this myself because everyone else is sleeping and this is my responsibility? After all, this is my temporally induced Mind experiment.

The option of killing the messenger is currently unthinkable. It's not harming me now and I sense it will not harm me in the future. But can I rest easy; actually get a good night's sleep before my extremely long day tomorrow, knowing it's lurking nearby?

Why does my test seem to be so much more difficult? Is it because this is a tarantula and not a bee? Or is it because it seems that my physical body is now threatened in an unexpected way?

After failing to receive a message from the spider, words from my last book surface.

"Thoughts will control us unless we control our thoughts. Since thought is constantly changing, forever taking on new ways of expression, it's possible to change one's circumstances just by changing thoughts."

Does this situation apply? Will the tarantula disappear or at least hide further behind the smaller bed? Can I turn off the light, roll over, and drift back to sleep without another thought?

Ego announces.

"No, I cannot."

Panic rises as I consider catching the tarantula with a towel to release it outside. It scurries back under the bed when I throw the covers off to get up. The spider is out of sight and now the thought of trying to catch it seems fruitless. I'm too tired to chase a spider around the room so I turn on the bright light in the ceiling. After relieving myself, I leave the bathroom light on as well. I pick my sneakers and slippers up from the floor to place upon the footstool thinking the tarantula will not climb its legs to reach them.

And then I get into bed, turn over to place my face away from the glowing light upon the footstool, and fall quickly asleep. The entities, I believe, will protect me.

Something wakes me an hour later. My face is now directed toward the footstool. I must have turned it while asleep. Intuition quickly guides me to look the opposite way, towards the wall to my right. The tarantula now sits directly in my line of vision a mere two feet from my face. Ah, the drama!

Can tarantula's jump? Did it climb under my bed and then up the wall to greet me? Or, eek, did it crawl over me?

There's no way to know and now it's a sure bet that I'm not going to sleep until it is gone. Despite everything learned over the past several years, and my reluctance to ask for help, I turn to the unseen for assistance. I still don't know if the tarantula's bite is deadly and I don't want to end up in a Brazilian hospital. Nothing, I fearfully decide, will stop me. I will return to the U.S. later today.

"Please," I announce to unseen entities in a whisper, "help me kill this thing."

Adrenaline pumps through veins but I remain at peace. My heart is almost, but not quite, beating normally. I get out of bed on the left side after grabbing a sneaker. The tarantula remains still as I walk around to the other side of the bed, skirt up the small space between it and the wall, and raise the sneaker.

"Thank you for your help," I announce to the unseen before sending the spider into the Light with a whack.

It falls to the floor and begins to squirm. I whack it again and go into the bathroom to get my single bath towel. Even though it's now dead, I still do not want to pick it up so I push the towel over to the door. The thin towel is not nearly enough to block anything else from entering the room. I now place the single bedspread near the door onto the floor to cover the gap.

At last, I can sleep.

Would unseen entities have helped to move a live tarantula from my room in the dead of night? I'll never know.

Shortly after dawn, I rise to start the day. It's now 6:30 AM.

Our tour bus driver greets the group in front of the Pousada after the usual breakfast. Maria stands filled with hesitation while she tells everyone goodbye. A small, beautiful white butterfly, with exquisite markings, flies nearby. Before long, it lands directly upon Maria to sit below her breasts.

We stare at it in awe as tears slide down her face. Awesome sight to see, a butterfly that lands upon someone and sits there for minutes without a flutter. I have seen such a thing before but only when someone added sugar water to his or her finger at a Butterfly Farm. And then it was only for a fleeting few seconds.

"I don't know if I'm doing the right thing or not," Maria announces, tears still dripping down her beautiful face, "but I am guided to stay."

"Your confirmation is right there," I remark, with a grin pointing to the butterfly, "right under your nose!"

The butterfly sits quietly, as if glued to her top, as people photograph it. It is, I believe, still there when we pull away minutes later. Maria got her confirmation in a very big way. I suspect the entities made sure of it.

We head toward Brasília, the third richest city of Brazil, still talking about the butterfly miles later. Billy Deeter, our tour guide begins to explain a bit about the area before we drop Cathy off at the airport for her early flight. It seems like a long drive to get her there on time. Why didn't I notice the distance upon arrival? Disagreeable thoughts fill my mind. It saddens me to know a member of our group will not be on earth much longer. But I have done all I can to help ease fears without sharing this news. It's time to enjoy this part of the tour.

"All is well in the mind of one that never speaks of separation.

"Everything in your world exists in wavering forms of energy. You can see this energy move by paying close attention while on the cusp of sleep. Some people on your earth see this wavering energy throughout the day. They are ones with heightened senses, the ones many now follow to hear reminders of True Self, the One in which all here reside.

"Let not these days before your sway thought to the dark side of life for things again change greatly in

coming days. Many will not bear the energies of changing consciousness and shall leave their physical form.

"We know many now are aware of the fleeting forms here on your earth, the sanctity of life, as you refer to it. But many more are not. Those are the ones that will leave or change the most in coming days.

"All things on your earth exist in wavering forms of various degrees of Light. Those holding the least amount of Light now leave to play their game elsewhere. Those remaining have either chosen to progress or leave in times to come.

"You may count on one thing as the days on earth progress to an unrecognizable state for many. Change will continuously occur. Let this not dissuade you from the truth of your Self. All are part of **All That Is**. There is nothing outside the One of Truth, of Light, of Love. You and all others are that of which **It** is."

Details slip quickly away. I take very few pictures. At one point, we walk the granite, "anti-clockwise" labyrinth, sitting within the Temple of Good Will, under what many people refer to as "the largest pure crystal rock in the world." I don't even look up to see it but sense the unseen as Steve and I stop to periodically immerse ourselves in healing energies.

The blue, stained glass of Brasilia's Dom Bosco Sanctuary (Dom Bosco is Brazil's patron saint) astonishes, as does the Cathedral of Brasília, which we enter by walking down a long, concrete ramp. Vendors with local wares line the path before we descend.

The Cathedral of Brasília is a concrete-framed hyperboloid structure with a glass roof reaching up. It looks like two hands reaching to the heavens. Inside, three angels, of increasing dimension, soar down from the center as if to signify our descent into duality.

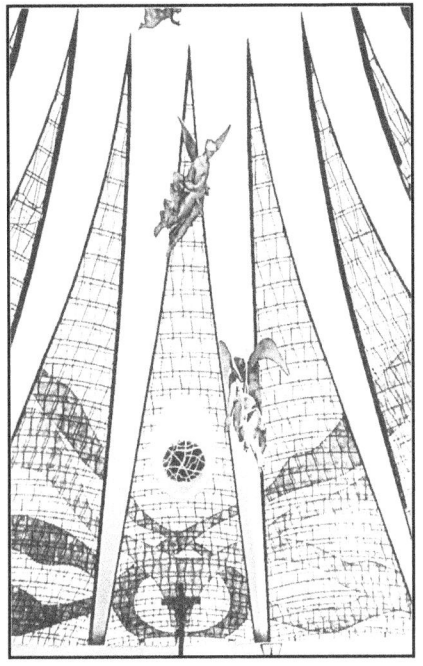

Stained glass in Cathedral of Brasília

We enjoy the most wonderful buffet lunch in Brasilia at a beautiful, open-air restaurant. An eggplant dish is like "a party in my mouth" as I savor the taste of eggplant, olive oil and rich, blue cheese. A furry of activity outside, where staff prepares for a wedding in the garden beyond the pavilion, contrasts the quiet dining room.

The Juscelino Kubitschek Bridge, a series of half-circles that crosses Lake Paranoá, soon offers a panoramic view of what some refer to as Brasilia's Beverly Hills. Except for Ernie, we have already dropped off the rest of our group at the airport. Now we drive past large, expensive homes lining the beautiful lake before leaving him at a hotel to wait for his later flight.

Steve and I board TAM flight 3563 to meet Cathy in San Paulo, Brazil for our flight back to Miami. It's now 7:30 PM and I'm beginning to tire. The Sao Paulo Guarulhos International Airport swarms with activity hours later as we wait for a midnight flight. It seems like a very, long, wait, in an airport filled with denser energies.

Our small group disembarks in Miami before breezing through customs at 7:30 AM on Sunday morning. There's no line to speak of so we easily move through the maze. I've been awake for twenty-five hours now and am beginning to get confused. Rev. Kent Barnard stands like a Light in the darkness as we make our way out of the airport. I'm so thankful he asked to drive us home.

After unpacking, I lie down expecting to transmute discarnate energies while napping. When I rise hours later, a bunch of what most people would call ant bites, but they aren't ant bites, sit near my ankle and calves, mostly on the right side. The marks bear an uncanny resemblance to the leg skin complaint mentioned by the young man in Brazil. I call them "transmutation rashes."

Sleep claims me again at 9:00 PM. Weird dreams fill the hours. A nightmare wakes me at seven o'clock on Monday morning. The now familiar force field around my body dissipates as I begin to rise. Now a big, what most people would call bug bite, sits on my throbbing, right index finger. It's painful and there seems to be a small seed in the middle of the red bump. My head is still spinning when I stand.

I'm beginning to think some dreams help to transmute discarnate energies from previous or even parallel, multidimensional lives. These human lives are blending, the result perhaps, of changing vibrational energy, within the sleeping physical form, to allow glimpses into other dimensions.

(As soon as I wrote this, a sudden, uncommon, demanding urge to use the toilet forced me to rise. It turned out to be one of those occasional times that I read the book sitting in my bathroom. The passages within Jane Roberts Psychic Politics *spoke of multidimensional lives, how we live more than one life at a time.*

Steve Rother, who channels what he refers to as "The Group" tells us our soul lives eleven imagined physical lives, at the same time, in what I think are parallel realities. We tap into those lives when our state of awareness changes. It sure makes sense to me now!)

Friendly energies surround me for almost an hour as I lay with the triangle on my forehead, repeating, "One Light, One Life, One Love" late on Tuesday morning. This force field is such a wonderful, wonderful energy, and it is good. My day is shorter than usual for it really feels as if I have had physical surgery. I am exhausted.

More weird dreams fill hours, and hours, of sleep. It seems that I'm living parallel lives. And in those lives, I'm not always as consciously aware as I am in this one. Most of the time, I'm not aware that this is an illusion and that I can change things. I usually don't talk to others as if I'm aware.

An unexpected guest greets me when I get ready for bed at the end of the day. Upon the bedroom carpet, sits a small, very skinny, perhaps three-inch long, black snake. It's two feet away from the bed and looks like it has a white underbelly. I'm not really sure what to make of it and cannot figure out how it got into the house, let alone my bedroom.

There's no doubt that I'll release it outside as I head to the kitchen for a wet paper towel. Somehow, I know. It's not deadly but some kind of blessing.

On Wednesday, continued exhaustion leads me to nap prior to taking the nightly shower before bedtime. Yet, I know, all is in Divine and Perfect Order. Ever grateful, I'm so looking forward to having the stitches removed by Casa energies!

Extreme thirst causes me to rise about every ninety minutes to drink water and eliminate it. Sometimes I wake while breathing heavily and quickly, thanking Casa entities and knowing it's part of the process. Aware of coughing up discarnate energies, I rise again, hacking, on Thursday, June 30, 2011 at 3:23 AM. Twenty-six minutes later I hear, "We are taking the stitches out now."

I'm on my right side as the force field surrounds me. It's unusually stronger than ones experienced previously.

"Can I move?" I ask, thinking it might be best to lie on my back.

"It is not necessary."

My breathing becomes quick and shallow.

"Thank you for writing the book. You will receive all the help you need. The book will do well."

And then, the process is over.

My mouth is as dry as the Sahara Desert so I drink the water sitting in a glass upon the nightstand. Both eyes are wet but the right one holds more moisture. Sleep claims me again after using the bathroom. Weird dreams, mainly of strangers, fill the hours.

Today's message, as the triangle sits upon my head and waves move throughout my body, comes upon waking for the day.

"All is well. Divine Order, Divine Timing prevails. Fear not."

Epilogue

Suffering may be useful for it leads us to the realization that it's unnecessary. Yet, everything, it occurs to me now as I finish this book, transpires for a purpose. Perhaps the "eye issue" manifested to prompt me toward John of God so I would document evidence of the unseen world that flows so freely within the small town of Abadiania, Brazil.

A channeled message published in *Lightworker's Log :-) Transformation* now comes to mind.

"*The form that represents us, is just one of many forms our soul takes on, to help us realize we are not really a form at all. We are Light, one of the bodies within the One Body of the Universe. Forms always appear and disappear within that which is changeless and formless. We are as formless as our Creator, One, living in a state of grace through the Power of God. Our reality is only Spirit, and we are in a state of grace forever.*

"*There are always circumstances that seem beyond our control in this illusion. These circumstances are not, necessarily, what they seem. There are ways to rid ourselves of these circumstances, and we must follow the tried, and true, method to do so. This method is the way we come back to the One, realizing that there is no limitation. That all are One, that we have never left, and shall always remain, in the bosom of the Lord.*

"*There are other ways to clear the emotions of dis-ease. These ways help us in becoming more alive with Source. These ways are the tried and true methods of the Masters. These emotional beliefs are not real. They don't fit into the mold. They are not a part of our natural self, for emotion is in itself human, and we are not human.*

"To let bygones be bygones is a source of truth. Follow the path of wisdom to the Master within. That is the truth of the nature of our BEing. That is the truth of the nature of All.

"Relinquish the past, forget the future. Live in the Now, knowing the Now moment is the only true moment. This will carry you through. This will secure you in the life you wish to live."

We can meditate all day long and stay in the awesome energies of Oneness but that does not serve the Whole by getting the word out that this world is NOT our true home. These bodies are NOT representatives of our true Self. We must live and breathe within the masses of the unawakened to complete our work here. We, I, must learn to take my comfort zone with me when called forth to serve and yet, there is nothing to serve!

Power lies within. The truth is, we heal ourselves with the power of Faith. For those totally unaware of this truth, the Casa is a Godsend. For those aware of their true nature, the Casa is a place of community offering many opportunities to boost their quotient of Light.

Epilogue

~ ~ ~ ~

Find more color photos of spirit energies in the Photo Gallery at the Lightworker's Log Website at LightworkersLog.com.

Perfecting the Light Body

Several messages within *Book of One :-)* and *Bits of Wisdom* (available through book sellers) note the importance of the Light Body. You may read them here as well.

Building the Lightbody

"The Lightbody is the only important body to concentrate on. We are developing these bodies now, mainly during sleep so it's important to sleep as much as one can. This is not an easy task for those of earth as all things fill your atmosphere with erratic waves of energy. Stay in places as far removed from these aberrant energies as possible to expand the Lightbody more easily.

"This is the Truth of your BEing, much more in line with the One of **All That Is**. Remember this in the days ahead as ego continues to pull you back into the illusion. Steer clear of old dramas now being replayed. Those that appear faced with such dramas must make different choices than before to reap a better future.

"Aberrant energies are rampant at this time. It is best to maintain a sense of the True Self to avoid their ill effects. Cleanse the body of toxic substances to do so. Stay away from synthetic (unnatural) substances and foods not from Mother Earth in their original form. Be clear about your path. It is the path back to Oneness in all aspects. You cannot get there by remaining in old dramas, old habits, old ways of thinking and living.

"Find new ways to nurture the Self within. Cherish those moments of solitude when you connect with the Truth of BEing and remain calm in the peace of **All**

That Is as much as possible. This is the Truth of your new being if you chose it.

"For others, the path wavers but always returns to One. Know this and be unconcerned for those wavering along the way."

Lightbody Activation

Clear your mind to experience this light activation fully. As thoughts arise, store them in a wooden ship that sits amid calm seas. Place all concerns and people that come to mind on the ship. Allow the ship to drift away while you take this journey into the sea of consciousness. You may choose to close your eyes and listen to this podcast at: LightworkersLog.com/videos/LightbodyActivation.wmv.

Feel a sense of lightness fill your body as you drift upon the sea of consciousness, as if lying on a float in the ocean. The seas are calm as your body rocks slowly upon the float. The ultimate Heaven, nirvana, lies ahead. There's a knowing that your float knows exactly where to drift as your body feels at peace with the elements of Nature. You soon come to a place of perfect union with nirvana, the supreme experience.

A huge shining circle beckons you forward. There's an arc of golden light that stretches to embrace you as you look into the circle. The circle fills with golden light before your eyes and then expands to cover everything, including you. The all-encompassing light embraces you in a perfect state of Oneness. In this state of BEing, you are aware of pure peace, yet exquisite emotion.

Perfecting the Lightbody

It is impossible to experience thoughts of separation. Nothing exists as a separate piece of matter. Everything is joined in perfect continuity within this Perfect Environment. Cozy warmth is all around you. It is of you and through you. There is no up or down as you float in warm soft clouds. Rays of brilliant Light, in ever-changing shades and hues, flow within the clouds. The pleasure of good fills your senses as each ray bathes you with its light. This nirvana is where you belong for it is Home.

All the colors of the spectrum continue to come and go. Each color brings a different relaxing or restful happiness. Ruby-red rays of light prompt meaningful thoughts of something beyond what you know as light. You move slowly and effortlessly through the cloud, listening to Music that surrounds you. The Music is around and within you. And you vibrate in harmony with *It*. You are a part of *It*, and *It* is you.

This purity of Truth is the longing, nostalgia, sense of destiny that you felt when you longed for Home, now fulfilled. You are Home where you belong. Familiar others are joined, bonded to you, with a great single knowledge of Oneness. They are you. You are they. Gentle waves of Love pass effortlessly between you, filling you with a completeness of Love. You are Home, where you belong, in perfect balance.

It is time to activate the Light of Oneness. Brilliant white Light now flows through every part of your being. You sense this Light, moving effortlessly throughout you. The Light is a familiar part of your True BEing and you welcome it with immense joy. It moves in waves, filling you with a sense of completeness, of Oneness with all things. This Light of Wholeness holds the memory of your Lightbody perfection. It is the Light you will take back with you to complete your earth journey. Bask in this Light now. Bask in the memory of your Lightbody perfection. You may activate this Light at any time you wish for this Light is you.

Now it is time to return to your float. The memory of how to activate your being with the Light of Home remains within as you drift upon the calm seas of consciousness. Far off in the distance, you see the wooden ship that houses all thoughts, concerns, and people left behind. Will you allow yourself to chart a new course? Is this the beginning of a new adventure? The choice is, and always remains, yours.

Inspiration derived from *Journeys Out Of The Body* by Robert A. Monroe.

Lightbody Expansion

"Refining the Lightbody is as easy as concentrating on the white sparks of Light within. One moves Light at a greater rate upon continued concentration. Let us begin to concentrate on this process.

"Settle into a comfortable position. It need not be sitting. Many find that lying on one's back in a straight position works well.

"Beginners may wish to start by concentrating on the Spirit spark within the heart, expanding that spark throughout the body in sequence."

(Lightbody Activation – free download at LightworkersLog.com/video/LightbodyActivation.wmv – may be more useful to do this.)

Perfecting the Lightbody

"Those already familiar with the concept of expanding the Lightbody do well by scanning their form to check for gaps in Light, filling and expanding the Light in less densely populated areas. Place more concentration on these areas while scanning the body.

"Let us begin for those ready to do so.

"If you now feel a vibration of energy throughout your physical form, concentrate on expanding it as we discuss each body part. If you don't feel the vibration just know that it's there. Let's start with the toes and work our way up.

"See brilliant, white Light, in the form of sparks, filling each toe from its tip, past the nail, to the beginning of your sole. Envision the Light pulsating upward slowly through the arch of each foot to move up the heel into each ankle. See the Light flowing as each spark of Light coalesces into one brilliant form of free-flowing Light.

"Move the flow slowly up each ankle to the knees, feeling the vibrating pulse of Light becoming stronger as it moves up. See the Light flowing up each thigh into the stomach, permeating the buttocks, now swirling into the chest to meet the main brilliant spark of white Light in the core of your heart.

"Your body feels more alive as this Light boosts its brightness, while flowing slowly up the chest and back, down through the shoulders to both arms and hands, and to the neck area. Feel each spark caressing the flesh as it moves upward, expanding beyond the confines of your skin.

"Your body is alive with this Light pulsating up into the face, up the back of your neck, and into your brain. The flow continues out the crown of your head and swirls down the sides of your body to reenter the physical *frame through your feet. It then flows up your spine in ever-increasing waves, continuing to feed the force of energy within as it radiates outward.*

"Your tube torus in now brilliantly fed with this life-affirming, luminous, white Light. Move it in a way that feels comfortable for you. Expand it to reach as far as you wish. Feel the tube torus continue to flow up out of the crown chakra, around the physical frame, back up the feet and though the spine as it again arches after flowing though the crown. Continue sensing this marvelous feeling of perfection, feeding it with the Love that you are.

"Return to wakefulness when you are ready to do so, knowing that this Light remains within. Sense it throughout the day and night to continue nurturing your body of Light."

About the Author

SAM is a wayshower helping others to learn the truth of their BEing so humanity can return to Source. She is a lifelong believer in the power of Love. Her inspiring life demonstrates the strength of Mind over matter. It is a story of progression from desperation to hope, poverty to riches, limitation to freedom, and fear to Love.

The awareness that we are spirits, in human form having a physical experience, came to SAM shortly after April 4, 2004. A quest for self-mastery began in 2005 when the essence of her son led her to the Science of Mind. SAM turned her back on traditional medicine after decades of illness and multiple surgeries. Using Eastern medicine, and the teachings of Ernest Holmes, she successfully rid herself of many maladies.

SAM's book series is a personal account highlighting the process of one Lightworker's awakening. Books from this author include:

Book One: Death of the Sun

Book Two: A Change in Perception

Transformation :-) Book Three

Prayer Treatments

Adventures in Greece and Turkey

Earth Angels

Return to Light John of God Helps

<u>Bits of Wisdom</u>

<u>Book of One :-) Volume 1</u>

<u>Book of One :-) Volume 2</u>

SAM is administrator of the popular Internet resource, Lightworker's Log (<u>LightworkersLog.com</u>). She currently concentrates on writing and spreading Spirit's message of Oneness. Guided by messages and synchronicities, SAM knows her most valuable asset is the ever-increasing awareness of our true BEing, unique figments of *All That Is*.